MANAGING STRATEGY

MANAGING STRATEGY

PROFILE BOOKS

First published in Great Britain in 2014 by
Profile Books Ltd
3a Exmouth House
Pine Street
Exmouth Market
London EC1R 0JH
www.profilebooks.com

10 9 8 7 6 5 4 3 2 1

A CIP catalogue record for this book is available from the British Library.

ISBN: 978 1 78125 219 2
eISBN: 978 1 78283 030 6

Text design by sue@lambledesign.demon.co.uk

Typeset in Helvetica by MacGuru Ltd
info@macguru.org.uk

Printed and bound in Britain by Clays, Bungay, Suffolk

All reasonable efforts have been made to obtain permission to reproduce
copyright material. Any omissions or errors of attribution are unintentional
and will be corrected in future printings following notification in writing to the
publisher.

About the checklist series

Management can be a daunting task. Managers are expected to provide direction, foster commitment, facilitate change and achieve results through the efficient, creative and responsible deployment of people and other resources. On top of that, managers have to manage themselves and develop their own personal skills. Just keeping up is a challenge – and we cannot be experts in everything.

The checklists in this series have been developed over many years by the Chartered Management Institute (CMI) to meet this challenge by addressing the main issues that managers can expect to face during their career. Each checklist distils good practice from industry to provide a clear and straightforward overview of a specific topic or activity, and has been reviewed by CMI's Subject Matter Experts Panel to reflect new research and changes in working life.

The series is designed both for managers who need an introduction to unfamiliar topics, and for those who want to refresh their understanding of the salient points. In more specialised areas – for example, financial management – checklists can also enable the generalist manager to work more effectively with experts, or to delegate more effectively to a subordinate.

Why is the checklist format useful? Checklists provide a logical, structured framework to help professional managers deal with an increasingly complex workplace – they help shape our thoughts and save us from being confused by too much information. At the same time, checklists help us to make good use of what we already know. They help us to remember things and prevent us from forgetting something important. Thus, no matter how expert we may already be, using checklists can improve outcomes and give us the confidence to manage more effectively, and to get the job done.

About this book

This book is aimed at anyone who is seeking a practical introduction to organisational strategy. Using a combination of action-oriented checklists and handy short summaries of the ideas of seminal management thinkers, *Managing Strategy* explains what to do and what to avoid. The checklists take you logically through a journey, starting with helping you to understand your organisation and carry out strategic analysis, through to guidance on evaluating strategic options, implementing your strategy, and measuring and evaluating its success. Along the way there are handy guides to objective setting, the balanced scorecard, decision making and the role of the board. This concise and indispensable handbook finally lays out the dos and don'ts of various strategic options, such as mergers and acquisitions, strategic partnering and deciding whether to outsource.

Contents

Measuring and evaluating strategy

Strategic options

Introduction

Strategy is a word of only eight letters. Yet those eight letters are the making or breaking of many a manager. Originating and forming a well-honed strategy, articulating it well enough to gain the necessary commitment, and then implementing, monitoring and adapting it tests a wide range of management skills and characteristics. Not least our judgement and interpersonal skills, as well as our fundamental strength of character.

Effective managers who can turn a vision into a successful reality, whether it was their vision or not, do so through having a robust and well-executed strategy. As I once put it to a rampant entrepreneur who was long on ideas and short on action, 'Strategy is a vital connection between the dream and the money, but that connection is only possible if the strategy is realistic and the resources are in place to implement it.'

Few people can combine the talents of the visionary, the strategist and the implementer. Smart leaders know this as well as they know where their own talents lie. They know their managers well, and they build teams that collectively can complement them in order to turn their dreams into thriving organisations. This is as true in a business as it is in social enterprise or a government department.

The difficulty of getting strategy right and the absence of 'one right way' to decide on the best strategy might explain why levels of interest in 'strategy' and 'strategy-making' continue to be so high. Gurus on the topic – such as Michael Porter, Henry

Mintzberg, Gary Hamel and C. K. Prahalad – have long grappled with the question of why some organisations are more successful than others. A steady stream of books and articles continues to be published as old models of strategy-making are critiqued and new ideas emerge.

There are many definitions of strategy, including the CMI's own simple one: 'The direction an organisation takes with the aim of achieving business success in the long term.'

This resonates with Alfred D. Chandler's classic: 'The determination of the basic long-term goals and objectives of an enterprise, and the adoption of courses of action and the allocation of resources necessary for carrying out these goals.'[1]

If you want to go back further, the term strategy is derived from the Greek *strategia*, meaning 'generalship'. It was originally used in the context of warfare to describe the overall planning of a campaign, as opposed to the tactics. Indeed, before business publishing came to claim the word, writers on strategy tended to focus on lessons drawn from the achievements of legendary military leaders ranging from Sun Tzu, a Chinese general from the time of Confucius, and the Prussian general Carl von Clausewitz to the British naval hero Horatio Nelson.

The word strategy was reportedly first applied to business after the Second World War. However, it was the landmark publication in 1965 of Igor Ansoff's book *Corporate Strategy*[2] which led to the development of a systematic approach to strategy formulation and strategic decision-making. This evolved into the structured discipline of strategic planning which sought to set objectives and produce strategic plans to be followed by the organisation for the coming year and beyond.

The basic model rested on a formal process of:

- appraising the external and internal environments
- using a range of analytical and forecasting tools
- choosing a strategy based on the results of the analysis
- setting objectives

- producing a plan to meet them
- implementing the plan
- monitoring progress in achieving objectives.

Strategic planning, it was argued, could be effective in a stable environment, and it was seen as a rigorous, scientific and evidence-based approach.

This approach had its heyday during the 1960s and 1970s, but as the twentieth century progressed, the economic and business environment became increasingly characterised by change, uncertainty and volatility, and criticisms of strategic planning started to be voiced. From the manager's perspective, strategic planning was time-consuming but often seemed to produce little in the way of results. The exercise often appeared to be more about streamlining and controlling what was already in place than about identifying new directions and opportunities.

With significant growth in the 1980s in both international trade and the importance of global brands, Michael Porter shifted the focus onto the competitive aspect: 'Competitive strategy is about being different. It means deliberately choosing a different set of activities to deliver a unique mix of value.'[3]

Then in the next decade significant challenges were posed by writers such as Henry Mintzberg. In his 1994 book *The Rise and Fall of Strategic Planning*[4] Mintzberg questioned the underlying assumption that there could be 'one right answer' to questions about strategy. He then went on to criticise strategic planning for its bureaucracy, inflexibility and tendency to stifle innovation.

As the technology and communications revolution in the 1990s and first decade of this century developed, culminating in the internet age, such processes were considered by many to be outdated; when circumstances were liable to alter so dramatically before a plan could be implemented, planning seemed redundant. Yet the chaos of the early internet age and the bursting of the dot.com bubble perhaps suggested that a 'random walk' approach to strategy may also not be great.

For some the 'emergent strategy' is a natural and pragmatic compromise, in which strategy essentially evolves from everyday activities and decisions, through a process of experimentation and learning or as a result of political dynamics within the organisation. As decisions are taken, a pattern that sets strategic direction for the future becomes clear. In my view this approach requires exceptional talent and leadership to be successful.

And that is probably why most organisations still use some kind of structured process for developing strategy. It is still important to be aware of the external business environment, to have an understanding of markets, competitors and customers, and to know what your organisation is currently capable of. But this now comes with a greater emphasis on strategic thinking with the aim of generating, evaluating and selecting the most promising strategic options, and a keen awareness of the need to build in enough flexibility to allow for adjustments and realignments as these become necessary.

Looking at the latest thinking, and incorporating into it an element of sustainability, Vaughan Evans, in his 2013 book *Key Strategy Tools*, puts it as follows: 'Strategy is how a company achieves its goals by deploying its scarce resources to gain a sustainable competitive advantage.'[5]

Efforts are understandably made to distinguish strategy from the related concepts of vision, mission or objectives. Put simply:

- *Vision statements* encapsulate aspirations for the future; they present an image of where the organisation would like to see itself in the future

- *Mission statements* outline the overall purpose of the organisation, which it aims to fulfil

- *Objectives* are specific targets whose achievement will enable the organisation to realise its vision and mission.

Whatever your precise definition of strategy it will usually come down to making choices amid a degree of uncertainty and using information which is of variable quality. We live in a dynamic and fast-moving business environment. That's one of the things that make business today so exciting and create so much opportunity. Yet, as anyone in a management position the day after the Lehman's crisis in 2008 can tell you, it can also be pretty scary. So no matter how much market intelligence we have or how sophisticated our forecasting tools may be, strategic decisions are generally taken in a context of uncertainty.

Recognition of an increased frequency and amplitude of major changes and external factors has led to a move away from more rigid planning cycles and plans. The old five-year strategic plan ritual is giving way to plans which 'bake in' adaptability and are more 'step and contingency' based. It is therefore vital to monitor organisational performance, keep right on top of the market, track what competitors are up to, look out for emerging social or technological trends, and generally be on the alert for any changes which require a strategic response, be it a slight shift of focus or a more radical change of direction.

Strong strategic processes also involve testing the vision to ensure that there is a way of achieving it and that it will deliver enough success for the investment, time and risk entailed and be better than competing alternatives. The best processes avoid developing strategy in a vacuum and take account of competitor reactions and likely changes in environment.

Frequently the winning strategy will take longer to bear fruit than originally anticipated. Star managers have the conviction and courage to continue to pursue their strategies and bring all those necessary along with them. They will also have the ability to recognise when the strategy is no longer appropriate, face reality, and possibly – given enough courage – risk loss of face by making a required shift in time.

Responsibility for organisational strategy-making lies primarily with senior management and the board of directors. But managers at the middle and lower levels of an organisation, and indeed all employees, are concerned with implementing and acting on the strategy which has been set, and may also be involved in shaping and participating in the process of strategy development. This book aims to help managers, in particular middle managers, to gain an understanding of strategic issues and introduces some tools which will assist them in assessing strategic options.

There are many books on strategy, ranging from extensive textbooks to personal reflections, for those who have the time and the interest to read them, and there are also many different models of and approaches to strategy. It is not a subject that can be comprehensively addressed by means of short checklists. But what checklists can offer is a valuable introduction to the complexities of a subject in a straightforward and accessible format. The aim of this book is to provide insights and a range of tools and techniques that will help managers to engage with the development of strategy in their organisations and participate in the planning and execution of strategy in their own area of responsibility.

Latterly, more attention has been paid to how strategy is implemented or executed, as highlighted by Ram Charam and Larry Bossidy in their book *Execution: the Discipline of Getting Things Done*.[6] No matter how good a strategy, it is useless unless it is implemented, and its aims will never be achieved unless it is acted on and put into practice by engaging people right across the organisation. This approach is reflected in this collection of checklists.

The first section of this book focuses on the organisational context in which strategy is formulated and executed; the second examines the area of strategic analysis and introduces a number of commonly used tools and techniques; and the third section moves on to the meat of formulating and implementing strategy. A further brief section looks at evaluating progress in achieving strategic aims and objectives. This is followed by a final section exploring a range of strategic options that an organisation may choose.

Patrick Dunne
Member, General Council, The University of Warwick

Notes

1. Alfred D. Chandler, *Strategy and Structure: Chapters in the History of American Enterprise*, MIT Press, 1963, p. 13.

2. Igor H. Ansoff, *Corporate Strategy: An Analytic Approach to Business Policy for Growth and Expansion*, McGraw-Hill, 1965.

3. Michael Porter, 'What is strategy?', *Harvard Business Review*, November/December 1966, p. 60.

4. Henry Mintzberg, *The Rise and Fall of Strategic Planning*, Prentice Hall International, 1994.

5. Vaughan Evans, *Key Strategy Tools: The 80+ Tools for Every Manager to Build a Winning Strategy*, Pearson Education, 2013.

6. Ram Charan and Larry Bossidy, *Execution: The Discipline of Getting Things Done*, Random House, 2002.

Understanding organisational culture

Organisational culture is the way that things are done in an organisation, the unwritten rules that influence individual and group behaviour and attitudes. Organisational culture is defined by the organisation's structure, the behaviour and attitudes of its employees, and the management and leadership style adopted by its managers. Organisational culture reflects the personality and character of the organisation, and is composed of the values, beliefs and basic assumptions that are shared by members of an organisation.

An understanding of organisational culture is crucial for effective leadership. Leaders and managers will be better placed to implement strategy and achieve their goals if they understand the culture of their organisation. Strategies that are inconsistent with organisational culture are more likely to fail, while strategies that are in line with it are more likely to succeed. It is also important to understand the existing culture of an organisation before thinking about change.

The workforce of an organisation swiftly comes to understand its particular culture. Culture is a concept that may be difficult to express plainly, but everyone knows it when they see it. For example, the culture of an informal software company may be quite different from that of a large financial corporation and different again from that of a hospital or a university.

To gain an understanding of the culture of an organisation, the relationships between values, behaviour and unwritten rules must be examined. This checklist outlines the main steps and questions to ask to help gain this understanding. Some well-known methods used to classify organisational culture are also introduced.

Organisations are human communities, peopled with individuals. Once managers develop an understanding of why people and their organisation behave as they do, they will be able to improve effectiveness, communication, organisation, control and, ultimately, results.

Action checklist

1 Read

For example:

- the mission statement, in which the organisation's goals and values are explicitly stated
- publications, reports and newsletters – consider what is mentioned, emphasised or omitted and how the organisation presents itself
- the organisation's website and intranet.

2 Ask questions

Ask people who work for the organisation:

- what their impressions of the organisation are
- what words they would use to describe the organisation (e.g. professional, experienced, friendly, stable, secure)
- what sort of behaviour is expected of employees
- whether the message they get about the culture is consistent across all levels and units within the organisation.

3 Observe the physical environment

- Do the furnishings and decor make a particular statement?

- Are the surroundings formal or informal?
- How do people dress? Do they dress differently depending on their position within the organisation?

4 Assess communication styles

- How do staff communicate with one another (face-to-face, phone, email)?
- How do people address one another in the organisation, and how are superiors addressed?
- If a manager's office door is closed, how do people react and approach the individual?
- How accessible or approachable are senior staff members?
- How are organisational decisions communicated to staff?
- Is feedback (positive or negative) given regularly?

5 Look at the nature of decision-making and the impact on stakeholders

- How are HR policies such as remuneration implemented in practice?
- What level of priority and attention is given to customer service, and how are customer concerns or complaints handled?
- How are statutory regulations being applied?
- How is the balance between customer and business benefit handled when specifying products?
- How are accounts and financial reports managed?

6 Consider timekeeping

- Does the organisation operate with fixed working hours?
- What time do people come to work and do they arrive on time?
- Are coffee or tea breaks taken? Do they become extended breaks?

- Do people work their set hours only or do they stay late?

7 Analyse groups and networks

- Do people seem to prefer working in groups or individually?
- Do people gather together at lunch?
- Do people socialise at work, or outside the workplace?
- Do subcultures exist within departments or within professional groups?
- Are people encouraged to work outside their department or silo?

8 Observe dress codes

- Do people dress formally or informally?
- Are there dress-down days?
- How do people dress for special appointments or meetings?

9 Think about meetings

- Does everyone participate in meetings?
- Are people encouraged to share ideas at meetings?
- Who speaks at meetings?
- What do people say if they arrive late for a meeting?

10 Consider organisational boundaries

- What types of positions do women and members of minority groups hold in the organisation?
- Is saving face important to people?
- Does the organisation have a sense of stability, or is there unremitting change?
- Is there a common shared language consisting of jargon and acronyms?
- How are new members of staff assimilated or inducted?

As a manager you should avoid:

● assuming that an organisation's culture can be fully understood through superficial observation

● believing that the values expressed, e.g. in mission statements, necessarily reflect the values actually practised by the organisation.

Classifying organisational culture

A number of management thinkers have studied organisational culture and attempted to classify different types of culture. The following approaches may be helpful in assessing and understanding the culture of an organisation.

Edgar Schein believed that culture is the most difficult organisational attribute to change and that it can outlast products, services, founders and leaders. Schein's model looks at culture from the standpoint of the observer and describes organisational culture at three levels:

● Organisational attributes that can be seen, felt and heard by the uninitiated observer, including the facilities, offices, decor, furnishings, dress and how people visibly interact with others and with organisational outsiders.

● The professed culture of an organisation's members. Company slogans, mission statements and other operational creeds are useful examples.

● An organisation's implied assumptions, which are unseen and not consciously identified in everyday interactions between the organisation's members. Even people with the experience to understand this deepest level of organisational culture can become accustomed to its attributes, reinforcing the invisibility of its existence.

Geert Hofstede explored the national and regional cultural influences that affect the behaviour of organisations. He identified five dimensions of culture in his study of national influences:

- **Power distance** – the extent to which the less powerful members of organisations accept and expect the unequal distribution of power. This suggests that a society's level of inequality is endorsed by the followers as much as by the leaders.

- **Uncertainty avoidance** – reflects the extent to which society tolerates uncertainty, risk and ambiguity.

- **Individualism versus collectivism** – the extent to which people are expected to act as individuals, or as members of the group or organisation.

- **Masculinity versus femininity** – refers to the value placed on traditionally male or female values.

- **Long-term versus short-term orientation** – in societies that focus on the long term, thrift and perseverance are valued more highly than in societies that focus on the short term, where respect for tradition and the reciprocation of gifts and favours are more highly valued.

Charles Handy links organisational structure to organisational culture:

- **Power culture** – power is concentrated among a few with control spreading from the centre. Power cultures have few rules and little bureaucracy; decision-making can be swift.

- **Role culture** – authority is clearly delegated within a highly defined structure. Such organisations typically form hierarchical bureaucracies where power derives from a person's position and little opportunity exists for expert power.

- **Task culture** – teams are formed to solve particular problems with power deriving from expertise.

- **Person culture** – all individuals believe themselves to be superior to the organisation. The concept of an organisation suggests that a group of like-minded individuals pursues organisational goals. For this type of organisation, survival can become difficult.

Gerry Johnson and **Kevan Scholes** developed the Cultural Web in 1992. This is a representation of taken-for-granted assumptions of an organisation that helps management to focus on the key factors of culture and their impact on strategic issues. It can identify blockages to and facilitators of change in order to improve performance and competitive advantage.

The Cultural Web contains six interrelated elements:

- **Stories** – the past and present events and people talked about inside and outside the company.

- **Rituals and routines** – the daily behaviour and actions of people that signal acceptable behaviour.

- **Symbols** – the visual representations of the company including logos, office decor, and formal or informal dress codes.

- **Organisational structure** – includes structures defined by the organisation chart, and the unwritten lines of power and influence that indicate whose contributions are most valued.

- **Control systems** – the ways in which the organisation is controlled, including financial systems, quality systems and rewards.

- **Power structures** – power in the company may lie with one or two executives, a group of executives, or a department. These people have the greatest amount of influence on decisions, operations and strategic direction.

Charles Handy

Understanding the changing organisation

Introduction

Charles Handy (b. 1932) is well-known for his work on organisations. This has culminated in the formation of a vision of the future of work and the implications of change for the ways in which people manage their lives and careers.

His observation of work in modern society has identified discontinuous change as the (paradoxically) continuing characteristic of working lives and organisations. He has forecast a future – already with a good deal of accuracy – where half of the UK's workforce would no longer be in permanent full-time jobs.

It is Handy's understanding of the ways in which organisations are changing to meet the accelerating changes and demands of new and diverse markets that we shall concentrate on here.

Life and career

Born in Ireland, Handy is a self-employed writer, teacher and broadcaster. He is a visiting professor at London Business School (LBS) and consultant to a wide range of organisations in government, business, and the voluntary and educational sectors.

After graduating from Oxford, his working life began in the marketing and personnel divisions of Shell International and, as an economist, with Anglo-American Corporation. He then returned to academia at the Sloan School of Management of the Massachusetts Institute of Technology. In 1967 he was founder director of the Sloan Programme at LBS, where he also taught managerial psychology and development. Appointments as professor and governor of LBS followed in 1972 and 1974 respectively. In 1977 he was appointed warden of St George's House in Windsor Castle, a private conference and study centre with a strong focus on the discussion of business ethics. As a teacher he latterly concentrated on the application of behavioural science to management, the management of change, the structure of organisations, and the theory and practice of individual learning in life.

He is a former chairman of the Royal Society of Arts and in 1994 he was Business Columnist of the Year. He has been a regular contributor to 'Thought for the Day' on Radio 4.

Handy on organisations

Four of Handy's books in particular consider the structure of organisations in detail and offer a perspective on the way in which they work:

Understanding Organisations (1976)

The Age of Unreason (1989)

Gods of Management (1985)

The Empty Raincoat (1994)

Organisation structure

Understanding Organisations – described by publishers and commentators alike as 'a landmark study' – is equally valuable for students of management and practising managers. Among other subjects it deals with motivation, roles and interactions, leadership, power and influence, the workings of groups and the culture of organisations. They are considered both as 'concepts' and 'concepts in application'. A 'Guide to further study' points the way for further examination of each concept.

In *Gods of Management*, Handy identifies some established structures in organisations and suggests new forms that are emerging. He perceives that organisations embrace four basic 'cultures':

- **Club culture.** This is represented metaphorically by Zeus, a strong leader who has, likes and uses power, and graphically by a spider's web. All lines of communication lead, formally or informally, to the leader. Such organisations display strength in the speed of their decision-making; their potential weakness lies in the calibre of the 'one-man bands' running them.

- **Role culture.** This is personified as Apollo, the god of order and rules, represented by a Greek temple. Such organisations are based on the assumptions that people are rational, and that roles can be defined and discharged with clearly defined procedures. They display stability and certainty, and have great strength in situations marked by continuity; they often display weakness in adapting to, or generating, change.

- **Task culture.** This is likened to Athena, the goddess of knowledge, and is found in organisations where management is concerned with solving a series of problems. The structure is represented by a net, resources being drawn from all parts of the organisation to meet the needs of current problems. Working parties, subcommittees, taskforces and study groups are formed on an ad hoc basis to deal with problems. This type of culture is seen to advantage when flexibility is required.

- **Existential culture.** This is represented by Dionysus, the god of wine and song, and is found in organisations that exist to serve the individual, and where individuals are not servants of the organisation. They may comprise groups of professionals, such as doctors or lawyers, with no 'boss', and coordination may be provided by a committee of peers. Such structures are becoming more common as more conventional organisations increasingly contract out work to professionals and specialists whose services are used only as and when required.

The changing organisation

The link between this analysis of organisation structures and Handy's later work is, in part, provided by the development of 'contracting out' – one of a number of changes which he observes in the world of employment. Another major change is the basing of the quest for profit on intelligence and professional skills rather than on manual work and machines. Yet another is that the days of working for one employer and/or in one occupation may be over.

The shamrock organisation

An example of Handy's changing perception of organisations is provided by his use, in *The Age of Unreason*, of the shamrock to demonstrate three bases on which people are often employed and organisations are often linked. People linked to an organisation are starting to fall into three groups, each with different expectations of the organisation, and each managed and rewarded differently:

- The first group is a core of qualified technicians and managers who are essential to the continuity of an organisation. They have detailed knowledge of the organisation and its aims, objectives and practices. They are rewarded with high salaries and associated benefits, and in return they must be prepared to give commitment, work hard and, if necessary, work long hours. They must be mobile. They work in a task culture, within which there is a constant effort to reduce their numbers.

- The second group consists of contracted specialists who may be used, for example, for advertising, R&D, computing, catering and mailing services. They operate in an existential culture and are rewarded with fees rather than salaries or wages. Their contribution to the organisation is measured in output rather than hours, in results rather than time.

- The third group – the third leaf of Handy's shamrock – consists of a flexible labour force, discharging part-time, temporary and seasonal roles. They operate within a role culture; but Handy observes that although they may be employed on a casual basis, they must be managed not casually, but in a way which recognises their worth to the organisation.

The federal organisation and the inverted doughnut

The concept of the federal organisation was first explored in *The Age of Unreason* and was expanded in *The Empty Raincoat*. In it, subsidiaries federate to gain benefits of scale. Federal organisations should not be confused with decentralised organisations, in which power lies in the centre and is exerted downwards and outwards. In the federal organisation the role of top management is redefined as that of providing vision, motivating, inspiring and coordinating; initiative comes from the components of the organisation. Handy observes and describes the principle of 'subsidiarity' – not handing out or delegating power, but ruling and unifying only with the consent and agreement of equal partners.

In *The Empty Raincoat*, Handy uses the metaphor of the inverted doughnut to demonstrate how those in the subsidiaries must constantly seek to extend their roles and associated activities. The hole in the conventional doughnut is filled by the core activities of the subsidiary; the substance of the doughnut represents a diminishing vacuum into which the subsidiary can expand its activities given the necessary drive, will and ability.

Portfolio working and downshifting

Following on from his work on organisational change, Handy studied the effects of such change on the individual. He coined the concept of portfolio working, where full-time working for one employer becomes a thing of the past. Embedded in this is the notion of downshifting – the idea that it is possible to exchange some part of income for a better quality of life.

Although Handy has said that more and more individuals will opt out of formal organisations and sell their services at a pace and price to suit themselves, he has also admitted that comparatively few may find themselves in a position to take real advantage of this. He argues, however, that there is much that organisations can do to help individuals get to grips with the new uncertainty. It was in discussion with the Japanese that Handy coined the 'theory of horizontal fast track'. In Japan, the most talented people are moved around from experience to experience as quickly as possible, which means their skills can be tested in different situations, with different managers and in different cultures. This helps them discover what they are really good at and provides a lot of experience.

In perspective

With his imaginative use of analogy and metaphor, the Handy of the 1990s moves us from the past into the future. He argues that federalist and shamrock organisations can be successful only if organisations are prepared to invest in their workforce and build relationships of trust.

Although he is as much concerned with individuals as with organisations, his messages are sometimes disquieting. In a later book, *The Hungry Spirit*, he assesses the effects of the competitiveness of capitalism on individuals, suggesting that people can become not only stressed but also selfish and insensitive. But his message is not confined to pessimism about the future. On the contrary, the new capitalism consists of intellectual property (know-how, not merely physical and financial resources); the new knowledge markets enable low-cost entry to those with 'a bit of wit and a bit of imagination'; and the new products of the knowledge world are not nearly as destructive of the environment as the industrial products of the past.

Handy stands apart from many other management writers through his breadth of vision, his setting of management in a wide social and economic context, and the sheer readability of his writing. He is also ready to modify his views in the light of experience and further thought (he has admitted that some of his expectations have been proved wrong). He is not merely an observer of change but increasingly a catalyst, forcing people to stand back from their daily routine, take stock and view the future through different glasses, acknowledge change and address its implications.

Understanding management styles

Management style is the way in which managers exercise their authority in the workplace and ensure that their objectives are achieved. It is about how managers plan and organise work in their area of responsibility, and in particular about how they relate to and deal with their colleagues, subordinates and team members. The principal components of management and leadership style are attitudes and behaviour.

Which personal style should managers adopt to ensure success? What is the most effective approach to managing the work of subordinates? These questions have been extensively researched and debated since the 1950s, and the general consensus has moved away from command-and-control styles of management and leadership towards more consultative and participative approaches. However, there is no single ideal, as the best approach may vary according to circumstances and individual characteristics.

Style is a personal matter, and it is important for managers to be able to discover the style that works best for them and adjust it according to the tasks at hand and the people involved. In his 2009 book, *Managing*, Henry Mintzberg comments on the importance of context in partnership with style and refers to a symbiotic relationship, where 'style matters and context matters, but mostly they matter together'.

This checklist introduces some models of management styles to help managers begin to assess and develop their own style.

Some models of management styles

This review, which is by no means comprehensive, covers some of the best-known models and provides some pointers for analysing management styles.

Rensis Likert

Early theories about management and leadership style focused primarily on behaviour – the manner in which authority was exercised. Based on research carried out at the University of Michigan in the 1950s, Likert identified four different styles:

- **exploitative/authoritative** – leaders have little trust or confidence in their subordinates, manage by issuing orders, and use fear and punishment as motivators
- **benevolent/authoritative** – leaders have some trust in their workers but treat them in a condescending and paternalistic manner
- **consultative** – leaders show trust and confidence towards subordinates, seek their opinions and ideas, but retain decision-making power
- **participative** – leaders trust their subordinates completely, seek and act on their ideas, and involve them in setting goals.

Likert's research suggested that consultative and participative styles were more effective, but he did not consider the context in which management was being carried out.

Theory X and theory Y

Douglas McGregor, working in the 1960s, believed that management style was determined by the manager's assumptions about human nature. Based on his research, he identified two broad sets of beliefs that he labelled theory X and theory Y:

- **Theory X** suggests that human beings have an inherent dislike of work and need to be controlled and directed if they are to achieve objectives. This leads to autocratic and paternalistic management styles.

- **Theory Y** sees work as a natural part of life from which people gain a sense of satisfaction. Workers can be motivated to give their best through respect and recognition. This leads to more consultative and participative management styles.

McGregor believed that while both styles could be effective, theory X management could lead to demotivation and low levels of performance, but theory Y management could produce high levels of motivation and performance.

The managerial grid

Working in the 1950s and 1960s, Robert R. Blake and Jane S. Mouton identified two drivers of managerial behaviour: concern for getting the job done and concern for the people involved. To demonstrate how an individual manager's style is affected by their level of concern for these two factors, they used a nine by nine grid. This shows five basic management styles:

- **Impoverished management** – little concern for either the task or people. This style involves little more than going through the motions, doing only enough to get by.

- **Authority-obedience** – a high level of concern for the task and a low level for people. This represents a controlling style, close to the traditional command-and-control approach, but runs the risk of damaging human relationships.

- **Country club leadership** – high levels of concern for people and low levels for the task. This is seen as accommodating; it may create a warm and friendly working environment, but to the detriment of getting the job done efficiently.

- **Team management** – high levels of concern for both the task and people. This is seen as the most effective style, with the potential for high achievement.

- **Middle-of-the-road management** – moderate levels of concern for the task and people.

This achieves a balance between task and performance but is likely to perpetuate the status quo rather than achieve notable success.

William B. Reddin's 3D theory

Reddin (1970) also focused on concern for the task and concern for people, which he defined as task orientation (TO) and relationship orientation (RO). He introduced the idea that particular styles might be more appropriate in some contexts than in others. Starting from four basic styles – related (high RO), integrated (high RO and TO), dedicated (low RO) and separated (low RO and TO) – he added a third dimension, depending on how appropriately and therefore efficiently the style was used.

Style	Inappropriately used	Appropriately used
Related	Missionary	Developer
Integrated	Compromiser	Executive
Dedicated	Autocrat	Benevolent autocrat
Separated	Deserter	Bureaucrat

The Tannenbaum and Schmidt leadership continuum

Robert Tannenbaum and Warren H. Schmidt took a different approach in the late 1950s. They looked at the extent to which a manager exerts authority or control and the extent to which subordinates have freedom to act on their own initiative. They represented a range of possibilities along the continuum and identified seven styles: tells, persuades, shows, consults, asks, shares and involves.

They further suggested that a good manager would be able to judge the capabilities of the team and move between points on the continuum accordingly. Over time, as abilities develop, the manager may choose to accord a greater level of freedom while retaining overall responsibility for the work.

Situational leadership

Writing in the late 1980s, Paul Hersey and Ken Blanchard further developed the idea that different situations require different types of leadership. They saw the willingness and ability of subordinates to carry out the tasks allocated to them as the main factor in selecting the most appropriate leadership style:

- **telling/directing** when they are both unwilling and unable

- **selling/coaching** when there is some competence but a lack of commitment

- **participating/supporting** where they are competent but unwilling or insecure

- **delegating** where competence and commitment are both high.

For more on the Tannenbaum and Schmidt leadership continuum and on situational leadership, see the 'Understanding leadership styles' checklist, pages 23–5.

Action checklist

1 Know yourself

Looking at the models described above, ask yourself where you fit in. Think about which styles you feel most comfortable with. What are your preferred ways of working? What motivates you? How do you communicate with your colleagues and team members?

You may, at this stage, wish to complete a diagnostic test or assessment (testing through HR, using a professional model, is generally recommended) or consult with colleagues you can trust, using the models described here to support your insight and judgement.

2 Look at your work habits

- How do you manage your time?

- How do you set work priorities?

- How organised are you?
- Do you focus on formal team and one-to-one meetings or do you prefer to manage by wandering (or walking) about?

3 Think about how others see you

Reflect on how your colleagues and team members interact with you. How do they react when you ask them to complete a task or comment on their performance? Look at times when things have gone well or badly and try to identify how your own behaviour contributed to the outcome.

4 Consider the context in which you work

What motivates your team members? What do they expect from you? The answers may vary depending on their age, educational level or cultural background as well as experience and familiarity with the work. What may be an acceptable management style for one person may not be acceptable for another. Consider also the organisation you work for:

- What kind of management structure is in place?
- How are objectives set and how is performance managed across the organisation?
- What are the accepted behavioural and cultural norms?
- Do you work in a high-pressure environment or are things more informal and relaxed?
- How well do you think you are fitting in?

5 Identify areas for adjustment or development

Think about your strengths and weaknesses and any problems that have become apparent. Are there any areas where you need to develop your skills, adjust to the team you are leading, or adapt to the wider culture of your organisation? Consider what you need to work on and decide how you will go about this:

- Can you get advice from your line manager or can you find a mentor with whom you can talk things through?

- Would structured training in skills such as time management, communication or presentation be appropriate?

As a manager you should avoid:

- trying to imitate others or squeezing yourself into a mould that works for others
- taking an inflexible approach to management and leadership
- riding roughshod over the accepted style and culture in your organisation.

Understanding leadership styles

Leadership style is the general manner, outlook, attitude
and behaviour of a leader, particularly in relation to his or her
colleagues and team members. This can be expressed in various
ways, including:

- what a leader says
- how they say it
- the example they set
- their body language
- their general conduct and character.

Although there are numerous suggested leadership styles, the
need to be authentic as a leader and to have a style that suits
you, your personality and the people you lead is widely accepted.
Adopting an appropriate style is likely to build a good relationship
between leaders and their team members, helping to establish
rapport, trust and respect. Conversely, leaders who adopt or
display an inappropriate style are unlikely to be successful in their
job. Some employees may become disenfranchised, disengaged
and uninspired when faced with a leader who lacks the self-
awareness and know-how to pick the right kind of leadership
style. Reflecting on how you lead is an essential aspect of being a
good leader.

Your leadership style is largely to do with how you deal
with people, particularly those reporting to you within your
organisation. In his 2002 book, *Leadership Styles*, Tony

Kippenberger suggests that in a less deferential and more egalitarian society there is a need for leaders to actively assess and improve their style in order to engage followers.

A shift away from manufacturing and heavy industry towards knowledge and service-based industries in the economies of many developed countries over the past few decades has also influenced leadership style. More collaborative and coaching styles are seen to be effective in encouraging the motivation and customer focus on which service industries depend.

You are likely to have to adapt your leadership style to a certain degree throughout your career depending on the type of organisation you are employed by, your colleagues and your working environment. An awareness of differing leadership styles can help you decide which is appropriate for you and your organisation. This checklist describes some of the most popular theories of and approaches to leadership styles before going on to explore how being aware and thinking about leadership styles can be useful in practice.

Some models of leadership styles

The Tannenbaum and Schmidt leadership continuum

An early contribution to the literature on leadership styles was made by Robert Tannenbaum and Warren H. Schmidt in the 1950s. They proposed the idea of a 'leadership continuum' consisting of seven stages, each of which involves a decreasing use of managerial authority alongside an increasing level of subordinate freedom. The continuum progresses from stage one, where the manager makes all the decisions and announces them to the team, to stage seven, where the manager permits team members to function and make decisions within pre-designated limits. The seven stages of the continuum are:

- make a decision and announce it
- 'sell' a decision

- present ideas and invite questions
- present a tentative decision subject to change
- present problems, get suggestions and make a decision
- define limits and ask the team to make a decision
- permit subordinates to function within limits defined by a superior.

These stages effectively describe different leadership styles. Typically, leaders will move through the continuum, giving more responsibility to their subordinates over time – assuming the subordinates are willing to follow the direction of the leader and are performing at a suitable level. Tannenbaum and Schmidt acknowledged that style will vary depending on the leader, those who are led and the situation, and leaders need to bear this in mind when choosing their style from the continuum.

Leaders may lose some degree of control as they move through the continuum, but it is important to remember that the leader is always ultimately accountable for the actions of the team. Therefore, moving through the continuum requires a significant level of trust between the leader and the team members. Contemporary leaders are unlikely to regularly adopt the first command-and-control style or stage, and in most cases it should be used only as a last resort.

Situational leadership

The need to take account of the context or specific situation within which a leader is operating was explored in more detail by Paul Hersey and Ken Blanchard. Their situational leadership theory followed on from the work of William Reddin, who developed a 3D model of management style, and has been updated and refined several times.

As the name suggests, situational leadership theory states that different situations call for different leadership styles. Leaders need to be ready to adjust their style to suit the context. This relates largely to the competence and development level of other team members.

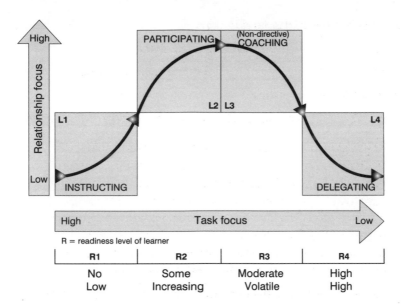

Figure 1: Situational leadership styles

Source: *Pathways Plus, Strategic Management and Leadership*, Level 7, 'Being a Strategic Leader' and 'Strategic Leadership Practice', Chartered Management Institute, revised 2010, page 69. Reproduced by permission.

Four leadership styles (directing, coaching, supporting and delegating) are classified according to the level of supportive and directive behaviour required in that situation. Supportive styles of leadership tend to involve two-way communication. Concepts such as social and emotional support, praising and listening are important. In contrast, directive styles of leadership tend to involve one-way communication from the leader to their colleagues and the focus is on providing clarity, goals and direction.

Further work on situational leadership by Peter Cumpstey and Philip Lindsay redefined the four styles as: instructing, participating, (non-directive) coaching and delegating. Figure 1 shows how these four types of leadership are affected by supportive and directive behaviour and the development level of followers.

Action-centred leadership

This is another situational approach to leadership made famous by John Adair. Action-centred leadership is perhaps more of an approach than a style, but it is widely taught and used by leaders globally, particularly in the UK.

Adair suggests that leaders need to be attentive to task needs, group needs and individual needs. The most effective leaders balance all three areas, as demonstrated by the Venn diagram in Figure 2. However, the leader may need to vary the degree of emphasis given to each of the three components in response to the situation at any point in time.

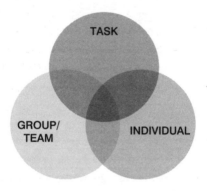

Figure 2: Action-centred leadership

Transactional leadership

In the 1970s and 1980s the transactional model of leadership was dominant. This is based on an exchange between leader and follower where the interests of both parties are served. The efforts made by followers to achieve organisational aims are exchanged for specific rewards, which may be financial or non-financial.

The idea of transactional leadership may lack the dynamism of other approaches, but it probably accurately describes the leadership practice in many workplaces. This kind of leadership can be particularly effective in emergency or conflict situations when all parties are able to see a tangible benefit.

Bernard M. Bass felt that effective leaders needed to exercise two transactional elements: contingent reward and management by exception. Contingent reward refers to the agreed exchange process between leaders and followers (e.g. leaders giving a salary or a bonus in exchange for the efforts and hard work of their followers); management by exception is characterised by corrective criticism and giving feedback when things go wrong.

Transformational leadership

The term 'transformational leadership' was first used by James V. Downton in 1973 and was popularised by James MacGregor Burns in his 1978 book, *Leadership*. It remains the predominant leadership approach in the literature and has also had a significant impact on the way that modern leaders behave.

Transformational leadership involves the engagement of followers and therefore transformational leaders are often charismatic. Accounts of such leaders differ, but most focus on how they can fulfil the development needs of their followers. In uncertain times, it has been suggested, employees want to feel inspired and empowered by their leaders, so transformational leadership fits well with the modern age.

A huge amount of writing has been devoted to transformational leadership over the past two or three decades, so the focus here is on the main thinkers.

Bernard M. Bass and Bruce J. Avolio

Echoing Tannenbaum and Schmidt's work, Bass devised a leadership continuum, from transformational leadership to laissez-faire leadership, with transactional leadership in the middle. For Bass, transformational leadership involved four factors:

- **Idealised influence/charisma.** Leaders are strong role models whom followers seek to emulate. They have strong moral and ethical principles and as a result are well-respected.

- **Inspirational motivation.** Followers are encouraged to do more than the bare minimum through the inspirational communication and high expectations provided by the leader.

- **Intellectual stimulation.** Leaders encourage followers to be creative and innovative, and to challenge their own beliefs and those of the organisation.

- **Individualised consideration.** A supportive climate is provided with coaches and advisers assisting followers. Delegation is encouraged to support the development of employees.

James M. Kouzes and Barry S. Posner

Kouzes and Posner describe five factors of excellent leadership that they believe anyone can learn to incorporate into their leadership approach:

- **Model the way** – be clear about your values and philosophy

- **Compelling vision** – create a vision that followers can use to guide both their day-to-day behaviour and their own dreams and visions

- **Challenge the process** – be willing to challenge the status quo and innovate

- **Enable others to act** – collaborate, trust and encourage others

- **Encourage the heart** – authentic reward and recognition are seen as important.

Warren Bennis and Burt Nanus

Bennis and Nanus identified the qualities of transformational leaders as:

- having a clear vision for the future

- being 'social architects' for their organisations – communicating a direction and form for their organisations that others can follow

- creating trust through consistency and clarity – making their position clear and standing by this

- having positive self-regard – having an awareness of their strengths and weaknesses, but concentrating on what they are good at rather than dwelling on their weak points.

All these authors see transformational leadership as being characterised by certain competencies and qualities. Common themes of these qualities include having a vision, having emotional intelligence, having charisma and being consistent and clear.

Authentic leadership

Recent corporate, financial and governmental scandals and misconduct have led to a growing interest in the related idea of authentic leadership. This focuses on being genuine, honest and trustworthy in your leadership style. For their followers to see them as authentic, such leaders must 'live their values', showing that they practise what they preach. An important aspect of an authentic leadership style is self-knowledge, although there is also a strong emphasis on knowing others and knowing your organisational culture. This enables you to strike the right balance between being an authentic, true version of yourself and fitting in to your company or organisation. Writers on authentic leadership include Rob Goffee, Gareth Jones and Bill George.

Action checklist

1 Know yourself

There are numerous questionnaires and tests that organisations and individuals can use to evaluate leadership styles. One of the most famous is the Multifactor Leadership Questionnaire (MLQ), developed by Bernard Bass, but there are many others available online and in printed form. For an in-depth evaluation of your leadership style, consider discussing your style with a trusted colleague or coach for a second opinion.

2 Know your team

Consider what kind of style would suit each member of your team. Their time in post and experience will influence how much support and guidance they need. Are they happy to be delegated tasks or do they need a lot of direction? If you are new in your leadership post, you may find that your team is used to working autonomously or that it needs a lot of guidance. Consider whether what has been done before is the best way forward, and which style will help the team with any new challenges or changes that are on the horizon.

You must be careful not to prejudge people, but at the same time take into account that there may be generational or cultural differences in some cases. For example, it has been argued that members of Generation Y (a term often used to refer to individuals born in the 1980s and 1990s) have different expectations of the workplace than the generation that preceded them (Generation X). It has been suggested that they are typically seeking fulfilment at work – not just a pay cheque – and therefore prefer leaders and managers who put time and effort into their development through coaching and mentoring. Today employees of all ages are likely to be less accepting of a command-and-control style and to want some input and a voice in decision-making.

3 Consider the context

A number of factors are likely to be crucial when considering the right leadership style for your organisation, such as:

- Is it a private company or a not-for-profit voluntary or governmental organisation?
- Is it currently doing well financially and/or succeeding as a company?
- Is it currently undergoing a lot of change?
- Is it a small start-up or a huge multinational conglomerate?

Many other factors are also likely to influence the kind of leadership style to adopt.

4 Share best practice with your team

Other people in your team may already be leaders or may aspire to a leadership position in the organisation. Even those with no leadership responsibilities or plans to take a managerial role at your organisation may be able to act as leaders, even in junior positions. Openly discussing the right kind of leadership approach to take and sharing your knowledge of leadership styles will be beneficial to everyone. You may be surprised by what the members of your team say they are looking for in a leader. Open discussion can also help clarify what people can expect from you as a leader and build rapport between yourself and your team.

5 Continue to evaluate your leadership style

Whichever leadership style you adopt, you are unlikely to stick with that style throughout your career. Take some time every few months to review your leadership style and consider whether it can be adjusted or changed for the better. Be prepared to vary your style according to the situation, rather than using the same one all the time. One of the most important aspects of leadership is the ability to reflect honestly and question yourself, so effective evaluation of your leadership style should contribute to better leadership practice.

As a manager you should avoid:

- failing to reflect upon the effect of your style on your colleagues
- sticking to one style rigidly regardless of situation and context
- not being authentic and true to yourself in whichever style you adopt.

Henry Mintzberg
A great generalist

Introduction

Often regarded as an iconoclast and a rebel, Henry Mintzberg (b. 1939) has certainly challenged many traditional ideas. But he does not attack people with whom he disagrees; he just quietly, simply and with devastating clarity sets about proving them wrong. In his writing, which is the product of a career devoted single-mindedly to understanding how people actually manage, he resists every temptation to pontificate about how anyone ought to manage.

Life and career

Mintzberg was born in Canada, and has spent virtually all his working life in that country. He studied at McGill University, and after further study at MIT, returned to Canada to take up an appointment at Canadian National Railways in 1961. In 1963 he moved into the academic world and by 1968 was back at McGill University as a professor, a post he still holds. He is also director of the Centre for Strategic Studies in Organisation at McGill and has held several important posts at other management institutions, including that of visiting professor at INSEAD, a French business school. He has been a consultant to many organisations throughout the world and from 1988 to 1991 was president of the Strategic Management Society.

Mintzberg's major impact on the management world began with

his book *The Nature of Managerial Work*, published in 1973, and
a seminal *Harvard Business Review* article, 'The Manager's Job:
Folklore and Fact', written two years later. Based on detailed
research and thoughtful observation, these two works established
Mintzberg's reputation by showing that what managers did, when
successfully carrying out their responsibilities, was substantially
different from much business theory.

Key theories

Unlike so many gurus, Mintzberg's contribution to management
thinking is not based on one or two clever theories within some
narrow discipline. His approach is broad, involving the study
of virtually everything managers do and how they do it. His
general appeal is further enhanced by a fundamental belief
that management is about applying human skills to systems,
not applying systems to people, a belief that is demonstrated
throughout his writing.

How managers work

In his *Harvard Business Review* article, Mintzberg sets out the
stark reality of what managers do:

*If there is a single theme that runs through this article, it is that
the pressures of the job drive the manager to take on too much
work, encourage interruption, respond quickly to every stimulus,
seek the tangible and avoid the abstract, make decisions in small
increments, and do everything abruptly.*

Mintzberg uses the article to stress the importance of the
manager's role and the need to understand it thoroughly before
attempting to train and develop those engaged in carrying it out:

*No job is more vital to our society than that of the manager. It is the
manager who determines whether our social institutions serve us
well or whether they squander our talents and resources. It is time
to strip away the folklore about managerial work, and time to study*

it realistically so that we can begin the difficult task of making significant improvements in its performance.

In *The Nature of Managerial Work*, Mintzberg proposes six characteristics of management work and ten basic management roles. These characteristics and roles, he suggests, apply to all management jobs, from supervisor to chief executive.

The six characteristics are as follows:

- The manager's job is a mixture of regular, programmed jobs and unprogrammed tasks.
- A manager is both a generalist and a specialist.
- Managers rely on information from all sources but show a preference for that which is orally transmitted.
- Managerial work is made up of activities that are characterised by brevity, variety and fragmentation.
- Management work is more an art than a science and is reliant on intuitive processes and a 'feel' for what is right.
- Management work is becoming more complex.

Mintzberg places the ten roles that he believes make up the content of the manager's job into three categories:

1 *Interpersonal*

- **Figurehead** – performing symbolic duties as a representative of the organisation.
- **Leader** – establishing the atmosphere and motivating the subordinates.
- **Liaiser** – developing and maintaining webs of contacts outside the organisation.

2 *Information*

- **Monitor** – collecting all types of information that are relevant and useful to the organisation.

- **Disseminator** – transmitting information from outside the organisation to those inside.

- **Spokesman** – transmitting information from inside the organisation to outsiders.

3 *Decision-making*

- **Entrepreneur** – initiating change and adapting to the environment.

- **Disturbance handler** – dealing with unexpected events.

- **Resource allocator** – deciding on the use of the organisation's resources.

- **Negotiator** – negotiating with individuals and dealing with other organisations.

The structure of organisations

In his 1979 book *The Structuring of Organisations*, Mintzberg identified five types of 'ideal' organisation structures. The classification was expanded ten years later in *Mintzberg on Management* and the following more detailed view of organisation types drawn up:

- **The entrepreneurial organisation** – small staff, loose division of labour, little management hierarchy, informal, with power focused on the chief executive.

- **The machine organisation** – highly specialised, routine operating tasks, formal communication, large operating units, tasks grouped under functions, elaborate administrative systems, central decision-making and a sharp distinction between line and staff.

- **The diversified organisation** – a set of semi-autonomous units under a central administrative structure. The units are usually called divisions and the central administration referred to as the headquarters.

- **The professional organisation** – commonly found in hospitals, universities, public agencies and firms doing routine work, this structure relies on the skills and knowledge of professional staff in order to function. All such organisations produce standardised products or services.

● **The innovative organisation** – this is what Mintzberg sees as the modern organisation, one that is flexible, rejecting any form of bureaucracy and avoiding emphasis on planning and control systems. Innovation is achieved by hiring experts, giving them power, training and developing them and employing them in multidisciplinary teams that work in an atmosphere unbounded by conventional specialisms and differentiation.

● **The missionary organisation** – it is the mission that counts above all else in such organisations, and the mission is clear, focused, distinctive and inspiring. Staff readily identify with the mission, share common values, and are motivated by their own zeal and enthusiasm.

Strategy and planning

The relationship between strategy and planning is a constant theme in Mintzberg's writing and his views on the subject are perhaps his most important contribution to current management thinking. In his 1994 book *The Rise and Fall of Strategic Planning*, Mintzberg produces a masterly criticism of conventional theory.

His main concern is with what he sees as basic failings in our approach to planning:

● **Processes** – the elaborate processes used to create bureaucracy and suppress innovation and originality.

● **Data** – 'hard' data (the raw material of all strategists) provide information, but 'soft' data, Mintzberg argues, provide wisdom. 'Hard information can be no better and is often at times far worse than soft information.'

● **Detachment** – Mintzberg dismisses the process of producing strategies in 'ivory towers'. Effective strategists are not people who distance themselves from the detail of a business 'but quite the opposite: they are the ones who immerse themselves in it, while being able to abstract the strategic messages from it'.

- **Strategy** – Mintzberg sees this 'not as the consequence of planning but the opposite: its starting point'. He has coined the phrase 'crafting strategies' to illustrate his concept of the delicate, painstaking process of developing strategy – a process of emergence that is far removed from the classical picture of strategists grouped around a table predicting the future. He argues that while an organisation needs a strategy, strategic plans are generally useless as one cannot predict two or three years ahead.

Mintzberg further explores strategy in his co-authored 1998 book *Strategy Safari*. In an attempt to define what strategy is, ten schools of strategic thought are outlined with a discussion and critique of each.

In perspective

Mintzberg remains one of the few truly generalist management writers, and he has applied his ideas to management education, which he believes is in great need of reform. In 1996 he helped set up an International Masters in Practising Management, which sought to change the way in which managers are educated.

His work is so wide-ranging that different readers see him as an expert in different areas. For some people he is an authority on time management, providing some of the most thoughtful and practical advice on this subject; for others he is the champion of hard-pressed managers surrounded by management theorists telling them how to do their jobs; and for yet another group he is a leading authority on strategic planning.

For most people, however, Mintzberg is the man who dared to challenge orthodox beliefs and, through the scholarly presentation of research findings and some truly original thinking, changed our ideas about many business activities.

Stakeholder analysis and management

A stakeholder is any group or individual with an interest or a stake in the operations of a company or organisation – anyone who can affect or be affected by its activities. Stakeholder analysis is the process of identifying an organisation's stakeholders and assessing their influence, or how they are affected, so as to manage relationships with them.

Operational stakeholder management relates to each manager within their own division undertaking the stakeholder analysis in order to clarify priority objectives and initiatives to better manage the motivation, cohesion and allegiance of key stakeholder groups. Stakeholder management is as applicable to individual projects and programmes as it is at the organisational level, so stakeholder analysis can be used in these areas as well.

In the past few decades, companies have been managed with financial returns for shareholders as the priority. Stakeholder theory, however, argues that the interests of all stakeholders – not just those with a financial stake in a business – should be taken into consideration. Stakeholder thinking suggests that this approach will contribute to the success of the business and ultimately the interests of shareholders. The needs of each party should be respected and understood, and, where practical to do so, met. It is essential that the concerns of all stakeholders are taken into account in order to maximise the value of the organisation. Managers need to identify who the key stakeholders are to effectively achieve this.

The stakeholder approach has been traced back to the work of Robert F. Stewart and Otis J. Benepe, who coined the concept when they were both at Lockheed Aircraft in the 1950s and developed it together at Stanford Research Institute in the 1960s. Growing interest in the role of business in society has also contributed to the popularity of the stakeholder approach, which focuses on not just a company's internal processes but also the wider social context in which it operates.

The primacy of the approach of maximising shareholder returns has been criticised for business as well as social reasons. Experts on governance such as Bob Garratt, Gordon Pearson and the late Sumantra Ghoshal have pointed out that shareholders do not own the company; they own shares in the company and benefit from limited liability. It is only through an understanding of the contribution of different shareholders that we can identify the sources of profit.

The aim of stakeholder analysis is to provide decision-makers with information about the individuals and groups that may affect the achievement or otherwise of their goals. This makes it easier to anticipate problems, gain the support of the most influential stakeholders, and improve what the organisation offers to different groups and individuals and how it communicates with them.

Action checklist

1 Gather information

Involve people from across your organisation to ensure that you get a full picture of all stakeholders. Relevant information can be gathered through brainstorming sessions, interviews and literature or internet searches.

2 Identify stakeholder groups

Writers have identified various types of stakeholders. They can be internal, for example employees, managers, trade union members or departments, or external, for example customers or suppliers. A distinction can also be drawn between primary and secondary stakeholders. Primary stakeholders define the business and are crucial to its continued existence. The following are normally considered primary stakeholder groups:

- customers
- suppliers
- employees
- shareholders and/or investors
- the community.

Secondary stakeholders are those who may affect relationships with primary stakeholders. For example, an environmental pressure group may influence customers by suggesting that your products fail to meet eco-standards. The list of secondary stakeholders can be long and may include:

- business partners
- competitors
- inspectors and regulators
- consumer groups
- government – central or local government bodies
- various media
- pressure groups
- trade unions
- community groups
- landlords.

Stakeholder groups vary enormously according to the nature of the business. A public-sector contractor, for example, might list central or local government as a primary rather than a secondary stakeholder. A train or media company may list its industry regulator as a primary stakeholder.

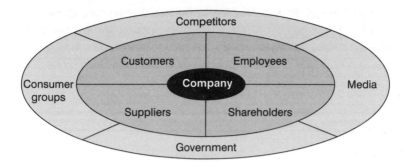

Figure 3: A stakeholder map

3 Map your stakeholders

One way to map stakeholders is shown in Figure 3, with the organisation in the centre, primary stakeholders in the first circle and secondary stakeholders in the second.

4 Be specific

At this stage, it is important to think about exactly who the stakeholders are and to name specific groups and individuals. Segment the groups where necessary. For example, list specific customer segments or divide your customers into retailers, distributors and end-users.

5 Prioritise your stakeholders

A power/interest grid can be used to map the level of interest different stakeholders have in the operations of your organisation and their power to affect or be affected by it (see Figure 4). This will help you decide where you need to invest your stakeholder management efforts. Clearly, you need to engage fully with those who have a high level of interest and a high level of power and develop good relationships with these groups. You need to keep those who have power but less interest satisfied, but not overwhelm them with information. Those with high interest and

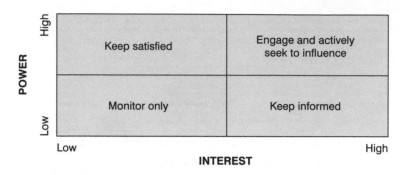

Figure 4: A stakeholder power/interest matrix

little power should be kept informed, but you do not need to pay so much attention to those with little interest and little influence.

6 Understand your stakeholders

Ask yourself what each stakeholder's perspective of your business may be:

- What are their needs and concerns?
- What affects or influences them?
- What do they believe?
- What motivates them?
- What potential threats or opportunities do they represent?

Consider what you know about their present and previous behaviour and what underlies it. It can be helpful to draw up a table listing each stakeholder and showing the level of priority you have assigned to them, the relationship you have with them and how they are affected by your organisation.

7 Develop strategies for action

Once you have decided which stakeholders you most need to influence and have begun to understand what motivates them, you will be in a position to consider the way forward. Here are a few questions to consider:

- How can you improve the products and services you offer to customers?

- Do you need to tailor your offering to different customer segments?

- How can you cooperate more effectively with suppliers?

- What will enhance the morale of your employees?

- What internal issues need to be resolved?

- What might encourage external stakeholders to be more cooperative?

- How can you change public perceptions of your organisation?

- Which policies or actions might run the risk of alienating them or increasing the threat they pose to your business?

- Which areas should you focus on?

Evaluate the impact of any proposals, considering how easy they will be to implement, taking any costs or cost savings into account and bearing in mind the impact on other stakeholders. Edward Freeman, Jeffrey Harrison and Andrew Wicks, authors of *Managing for Stakeholders*, suggest that trading off the interests of one group of stakeholders against those of another is a risky strategy. It may be more effective, although not easy, to find creative solutions that satisfy the interests of multiple stakeholder groups.

8 Communicate and develop relationships with stakeholders

A 'public relations' approach to stakeholders, i.e. one-way communication, can be used to put the company viewpoint across, but it will be effective only if the assumptions on which it is based are accurate. Two-way communication, involving dialogue and negotiation with stakeholders, may be more difficult, but it can lead to a better understanding of stakeholder perspectives. It can also foster your credibility with stakeholders and contribute to the development of relationships based on trust and respect, the resolution of conflicts and the evolution of win-win scenarios. Monitor the feedback you get from stakeholders and use it as a basis for further discussion and action. Stakeholder management is a two-step process, the second step being to develop a proactive communication plan aimed at supporting business strategy and seeking to move stakeholders towards supportive positions and away from positions that threaten business success. Moving stakeholders progressively in the right direction on the power/interest matrix should be the aim.

9 Monitor and review

The environment within which a company operates is not static. The power and interests of stakeholder groups will change, so a regular review of stakeholder relationships is essential.

As a manager you should avoid:

- assuming that you know what your stakeholders are thinking
- trading off the interests of one group against those of another
- ignoring the concerns of stakeholder groups that are critical of the organisation
- neglecting the interests of important stakeholders.

Gathering competitive intelligence

Competitive intelligence (CI) provides organisations with actionable information regarding competitors' plans, activities and performance and is a crucial part of an overall analysis of the operating environment. The information gathered (which can cover everything from new products, pricing structures and new recruits to overall strategic direction) is used to make both short-term and long-term plans in a number of areas, such as strategy, mergers and acquisitions, pricing, marketing, advertising, and research and development.

CI is both a product and a process:

- The product is information that can be used as the basis for a specific action (e.g. acquiring another company).
- The process is the systematic acquisition, analysis, evaluation and dissemination of information about known and potential competitors.

The effective gathering, analysis and application of CI can be a valuable tool, providing insights into the behaviour of current and prospective competitors and an understanding of the wider competitive environment. CI can support strategic decision-making, inform organisational positioning, build market orientation and help businesses to achieve competitive advantage.

In a complex and intensely competitive environment, where consumers are increasingly sophisticated and well-informed, it is not enough to collect information about the activities of competitors on an informal or ad hoc basis. Although conversations with clients and industry contacts and information from the media can be useful sources of intelligence, it is also important to take a more proactive, thorough and structured approach to CI. This can help organisations to minimise surprises, exploit opportunities and manage threats. Plans can be formulated on the basis of hard information and the organisation can learn from its competitors.

There are ethical and unethical approaches to gathering CI. Publicly available information from sources such as press releases, annual reports, job advertisements and the internet poses few ethical questions. However, sending employees to job interviews at competitor organisations is questionable. Business espionage using methods such as electronic surveillance and hacking is highly unethical and in most cases illegal.

This checklist provides guidance for individuals or organisations wishing to take a structured and proactive approach to gathering CI as part of a wider programme of market and environmental analysis.

Action checklist

1 Integrate CI into a single system

CI should be integrated into a central organisational system for the storage and retrieval of information. Make sure that information gathered by different departments and functions is fed into a single market and competitor database so that it is available to those responsible for strategic analysis and decision-making. In an integrated system, comprehensive reports can be produced and data can be optimally used for strategic purposes as well as at the operational level.

This may be achieved through an organisational market information and knowledge management system or a wider management information system (MIS) encompassing information derived from:

- **the internal accounting system** – especially sales analysis
- **market intelligence** – information from external sources, including the media and industry reports
- **market research of all kinds** – this may include information on indirect competitors or alternative products that may affect your customers' choices. This research can be either generated internally or commissioned externally from specific research organisations or industry bodies.

The intelligence gathered as the basis of marketing research is usually referred to as data and can be classified as:

- **primary data** – information collected by means of a specific research programme
- **secondary data** – information that already exists, because it was collected as part of a previous research project or for some other purpose. Identifying relevant sources of secondary information, extracting the relevant data and analysing it are usually referred to as desk research. Some companies set up a dedicated team to collect and circulate CI or subcontract the work to specialist companies.

2 Gain commitment from top management and across the organisation

Formal responsibility for CI may be assigned to a specific department or individuals, but input will be needed from individuals and teams across the organisation if the gathering and analysis of data are to be carried out comprehensively and effectively.

Commitment from senior management is required to make sure that resources are made available, particularly as direct returns on investment may be intangible in the short term. Staff time to cover the effort (and costs) of collecting, storing, analysing and constantly updating the information is the major resource involved, and these costs need to be monitored and controlled. Costs will also be incurred for activities such as travel to conferences and exhibitions, searching online databases and subscribing to journals. Senior management commitment is also important in ensuring that CI is taken seriously and acted on. The benefits will not be realised if CI remains an exercise in data collection and information is not analysed and applied.

3 Define the objectives

The gathering of CI needs to be conducted in a planned and thorough manner. Some kind of logical sequence should always be followed. It is vital to be clear from the outset why the research is required.

Usually CI is required to help senior managers and heads of department with management decision-making. Whoever is responsible for carrying out the research must engage with these decision-makers to make sure that the relevant CI is gathered and that it is presented in the most appropriate way. This will ensure that the resources available are used wisely, not wasted on exploring the wrong market, the wrong competitor or the wrong strategy, thus generating poor, irrelevant or misleading CI.

A wide range of issues may need to be addressed, for example:

- attempting to find weaknesses within another organisation
- finding out what the competition is in a new market that the organisation is hoping to enter
- investigating a particular organisation that is seen to pose a threat.

CI programmes should also include the provision of information for strategic decisions and early warnings of competitor activity. This kind of research would be wider and more generic.

Managers may wish to:

- focus in on their market and identify who or what constitutes competition for the organisation
- identify which of the many market forces is most important so they know where to focus their time and efforts

- understand which strategies their competitors are pursuing.

  You must clarify what type of data and information the CI programme will collect. Examples may include competitor pricing, competitor recruitment drives, competitor marketing communications – such as new advertising campaigns – and competitor strategy.

  In summary, clear and specific objectives for the CI programme will provide a focus and help reduce the amount of information that needs to be collected. The objectives should not be set in stone and must be reviewed regularly.

4 Develop the research plan

For example:

- Define the organisations from which information will be gathered. This could include competitors, peers, customers and industry bodies as well as suppliers.
- Decide on the survey methods to be used.
- Plan the approach in detail, working out a timetable and allocating human and other resources.
- Assemble the team and assign responsibilities. The number of people involved in the CI programme will depend on the objectives that have been set. One individual must be given overall responsibility for the CI programme; he or she must be a good communicator with strong information and project management skills, including the ability to work to deadlines.

5 Identify information sources

Some experts in the field of CI believe that most organisations already hold, or have access to, 80% of the information required to assess their competitors. Significant secondary data can be found within a company through its people and their current knowledge.

Additionally, many external sources of secondary data are

available, in government departments, trade associations, professional bodies, the press, specialist research agencies, academia and so on. Some research agencies operate syndicated research programmes that are set up on a cooperative basis and paid for by contributions from each of the companies taking part. It is possible to subscribe to such programmes. Alternatively, agencies sometimes commission research programmes and offer the results for sale. Trade associations often make information freely available to their members but sell it to 'outsiders'.

The techniques used to collect CI fall into four main groups:

- **Reviewing published materials and public documents** – annual reports, press releases, online databases and internet sites, the media, advertisements (especially competitors' recruitment advertising defining the kind of people they are looking for), product catalogues, other promotional brochures, and patents and trademarks.

- **Observing competitors or analysing products** – attending exhibitions and conferences, and buying their products and dismantling them as part of a benchmarking exercise.

- **Making contact with people who do business with competitors** – personal contacts in other trade organisations and existing customers.

- **Talking to recruits and competitors' employees** – job interviews with candidates working with competitors, conversations with competitors' staff at industry functions and networking events, direct contact with competitor organisations and making specific enquiries.

Do not overlook the importance of frontline staff as sources of CI. They are likely to pick up competitor information through dealing with customers. Make them aware of the need to keep a lookout for information and put in place procedures to gather the information.

Remember that all this information should be put into an

integrated marketing information system that is constantly being updated.

6 Develop an international perspective

Remember that language and cultural differences may limit cross-border intelligence gathering. It is not easy to approach competitors' employees, and people are particularly wary if approached by someone from a different country. Moreover, bear in mind that activities that are acceptable in one country might be illegal in another.

The cardinal rule of international corporate intelligence is that the best international competitor intelligence resource is your own organisation.

Most CI is probably available within your organisation. Even if it does not have offices overseas, you may have contacts worldwide through trade representatives, affiliates and suppliers. You need to appreciate that your organisation – particularly if it is globally based – possesses all three informational dimensions: competitor-specific; product- or technology-specific; and region- or country-specific. Be careful to take all three dimensions into account, not just two. For example, a sales person may know a great deal about a particular competitor or a specific technology but will also possess region or country knowledge.

7 Make the best use of technology

Technology can be used in two ways:

- **Gathering research.** Online databases and the internet are useful intelligence tools because they provide 'instant research'. However, they have limitations. The information may be out of date, inaccurate, biased and/or incomplete, so this kind of research must be undertaken with caution. The source of the information should be validated wherever possible so that its reliability and authority can be assessed. The currency and accuracy of the information should also be checked.

- **Storing research and intelligence.** Using a database to store the information you collect will allow you to search for a subject or a competitor more easily. Be aware of copyright legislation – it is illegal to scan many documents, such as press clippings, into an electronic format, but you may keep references or the newspaper in hard copy.

8 Consider primary data sources

If information required for a particular CI research project does not exist as secondary data, you have to determine the best way of collecting primary data. There are three fundamental approaches:

- **Observation.** It is sometimes more informative to watch what people do rather than talk to them. This eliminates interviewer bias and pre-empts the problem of people not always remembering their actions clearly, especially trivial ones.

- **Experiment.** Simulating a real situation is often a better way of assessing likely future behaviour than asking people hypothetical questions. For example, if you want to know which of two possible packages shoppers would prefer, you can put them side by side in a real or dummy shop and see which one is chosen. Test marketing is an example of experimenting in order to obtain CI data, although it has the drawback of potentially alerting your competitors to what you are doing.

- **Survey.** This is normally associated with competitor market research. It normally involves asking a predetermined set of questions to gather information. These questions can have either fixed or free-form responses. It is important to make sure that the survey covers all the areas required.

9 Analyse the information

The concept of analysis can be intimidating and it is not uncommon for organisations to gather information but fail to analyse its implications for their business. The analysis and interpretation of the data are crucial for the production of effective competitive intelligence. The management guru Peter Drucker has said that 'information is the manager's main capital'. For this capital to produce healthy returns it must be converted into intelligence, and analysis is the means of doing so.

The analysis should attempt to fulfil the objectives defined in point 3 above. However, it is important to be aware of potential problems when analysing the data:

- **The data may be incomplete.** Despite a thorough data collection process, there may be gaps in the data. There are two ways to address this issue – either further research is commissioned, or, if this is not possible, these gaps need to be highlighted and any assumptions used to fill them clearly explained.

- **The data may contain contradictions.** Again there are two options – further research is commissioned or these contradictions are highlighted in the analysis.

- **The sample size was not large enough.** If you are trying to gather competitor analysis, it may not be possible to collect data on all your competitors. This could skew the analysis, so any issues with sample size should be documented.

10 Compile a report

The report should clearly meet the objectives defined in point 3 above. It should also clearly state any problems or gaps in the data and the assumptions made during the analysis.

Brevity is important when reporting the information gained from the CI programme. Keep the intended audience in mind; highlight the most important points and provide references to further information.

Decide how often a report should be produced (weekly, monthly or even annually may suffice in some organisations whereas others may require daily reports). Frequency is based on the speed of change in the market in which you are operating.

11 Consider competitor responses

When considering actions as a result of the findings of CI, think about how your competitors will respond. There are four possibilities:

- **No response.** Are they weak or a sleeping giant? What if they wake up?
- **Fast response.** Some competitors may respond quickly and with such impact as to nullify your actions. What will you do if they do this?
- **Focused response.** It is possible that the competition will only change one variable (usually price). What will you do then?
- **Unpredictable response.** This is the most difficult to deal with, so what are your contingencies?

12 Take action on the results

CI gives a strategic advantage only when it is analysed and acted upon. Keep records of occasions when information was used successfully to gain advantage over competitors and also when it was too late to take action. This will help you improve the data collection and analysis process.

Do not jump to counteract a competitor's movements without considering your organisation's objectives. Only the right action for you, at the right time, will bring competitive advantage.

13 Learn and make changes

Monitor and evaluate the CI programme regularly and consider areas for improvement. Take action on any recommendations and keep communicating CI successes.

As a manager you should avoid:

- spending time and money gathering information that is no longer relevant to the organisation

- collecting data without analysing it
- overstepping the ethical line – check your organisation's code of conduct
- failing to communicate the success of the CI programme
- imagining that imitating competitors or beating them fractionally to market is the key to organisational success – seeking greater differentiation from the competition is a more effective route to a market advantage
- forgetting that competitors may also be trying to gain intelligence on your organisation.

Michael Porter
What is strategy?

Introduction

In an age when management gurus are both lauded by the faithful
and hounded by the critics, Michael Porter (b. 1947) seems to
be one of the few who are well-accepted both academically
and in the business world. Though he has his critics, Porter has
generally been viewed as being at the leading edge of strategic
thinking since his first major publication, *Competitive Strategy*
(1980), which became a corporate bible for many in the early
1980s.

Life and career

Porter completed a degree in aeronautical engineering at
Princeton in 1969 and took an economics doctorate at Harvard,
joining the faculty there as a tenured professor at the age of 26.
He has acted as a consultant to companies and governments
and, like many academics, has set up a consulting company,
Monitor.

Key theories

Porter's thinking on strategy has been supported by research into
industries and companies, and has remained consistent as well
as developmental. He has concentrated on different aspects at
different times, spinning the threads together with a logic that is
irrefutable.

Before *Competitive Strategy*, most strategic thinking focused either on the organisation of a company's internal resources and their adaptation to meet particular circumstances in the marketplace, or on increasing an organisation's competitiveness by lowering prices to increase market share. These approaches, derived from the work of Igor Ansoff, were bundled into systems or processes that provided strategy with its place in the organisation.

In *Competitive Strategy*, Porter managed to reconcile these approaches, providing management with a fresh way of looking at strategy – from the point of view of industry itself rather than just that of markets, or of organisational capabilities.

Internal capability for competitiveness: the value chain

Porter describes two different types of business activity: primary and secondary. Primary activities are principally concerned with transforming inputs (raw materials) into outputs (products), and with delivery and after-sales support. These usual line management activities include:

- **inbound logistics** – materials handling, warehousing
- **operations** – turning raw materials into finished products
- **outbound logistics** – order processing and distribution
- **marketing and sales** – communication and pricing
- **service** – installation and after-sales service.

Secondary activities support the primary and include:

- **procurement** – purchasing and supply
- **technology development** – know-how, procedures and skills
- **human resource management** – recruitment, promotion, appraisal, reward and development
- **firm infrastructure** – general and quality management, finance and planning.

To be able to survive competition and supply what customers

want to buy, a firm has to ensure that all these value-chain activities link together and fit, as a weakness in any one of them will affect the chain as a whole as well as competitiveness.

The five forces

Porter argued that to examine its competitive capability in the marketplace, an organisation must choose between three generic strategies:

- **cost leadership** – becoming the lowest-cost producer in the market
- **differentiation** – offering something different, extra or special
- **focus** – achieving dominance in a niche market.

The question is to choose the right one at the right time. These generic strategies are driven by five competitive forces, which the organisation has to take into account:

- the power of customers to affect pricing and reduce margins
- the power of suppliers to influence the organisation's pricing
- the threat of similar products to limit market freedom and reduce prices and thus profits
- the level of existing competition which affects investment in marketing and research and thus erodes profits
- the threat of new market entrants to intensify competition and further affect pricing and profitability.

In recent years, Porter has revisited his earlier work and emphasises the acceleration of market change, which means companies now have to compete not just on a choice of strategic front but on all fronts at once. Porter has also said that a company that tries to position itself in relation to the five competitive forces misunderstands his approach, since positioning is not enough. What companies have to do is ask how the five forces can help to rewrite industry rules in their favour.

Diversification

Instead of going it alone, an organisation can spread risk and attain growth by diversification and acquisition. Blue-chip consulting companies such as Boston Consulting Group (market growth/market share matrix) and McKinsey (7-S framework) have developed analytical models for discovering which companies will rise and fall, but Porter prefers three critical tests for success:

- **The attractiveness test.** Industries chosen for diversification must be structurally attractive. An attractive industry will yield a high return on investment but entry barriers will be high, customers and suppliers will have only moderate bargaining power and there will be only a few substitute products. An unattractive industry will be swamped by a range of alternative products, high rivalry and high fixed costs.

- **The cost-of-entry test.** If the cost of entry is so high that it prejudices the potential return on investment, profitability is eroded before the game has started.

- **The better-off test.** How will the acquisition provide advantage to either the acquirer or the acquired? One must offer significant advantage to the other.

Porter devised seven steps to tackle these questions:

- As competition takes place at the business unit level, identify the interrelationships among the existing business units.

- Identify the core business which is to be the foundation of the strategy. Core businesses are those in attractive industries and where competitive advantage can be sustained.

- Create horizontal organisational mechanisms to facilitate interrelationships among core businesses.

- Pursue diversification opportunities that allow shared activities and pass all three critical tests.

- Pursue diversification through transfer of skills if opportunities for sharing activities are limited or exhausted.

- Pursue a strategy of restructuring if this fits the skills of management or if no good opportunities exist for forging corporate partnerships.

- Pay dividends so that shareholders can become portfolio managers.

National competitiveness

Why do some companies achieve consistent capability in innovation, seeking an ever more sophisticated source of competitive advantage? For Porter the answer lies in four attributes that affect industries:

- **Factor conditions** – the nation's skills and infrastructure to enable a competitive position
- **Demand conditions** – the nature of home-market demand
- **Related and supporting industries** – presence or absence of supplier/feeder industries
- **Firm strategy, structure and rivalry** – the national conditions under which companies are created, grow, organise and manage.

These are the chief determinants that create the environment in which firms flourish and compete. They constitute a self-reinforcing system, and Porter represents them as the four points of a diamond, where the effect of one point is contingent on the state of the others. Advantages in one determinant can create or upgrade advantages in others. Similarly, weaknesses at one point will have an adverse impact on an industry's capability to compete.

The new strategic wave

Somewhere between 1980 and 1990 strategic planning came unstuck. Old theories no longer worked as customers became more demanding and changeable, and markets and technologies rose and fell ever more rapidly. Even industries that were once distinct with definable products and services now converged and became blurred. A new wave of more subversive strategic thinking – Gary Hamel in *Strategy as Revolution* and Henry Mintzberg in *The Fall and Rise of Strategic Planning* – emerged to replace the old rulebook. Porter's main contribution to date, *What is Strategy?*, argues that strategic planning lost its way because managers failed to distinguish between strategic and operational effectiveness and confused the two. The old strategic model – which still held up in the 1980s – was based on productivity, increasing market share and lowering costs. Hence total quality management, benchmarking, outsourcing and re-engineering were all at the forefront of change in the 1980s as the key drivers of operational improvements. But continuing incremental improvements to the way things are done tend, over time, to bring different players up to the same level, not differentiate them. To achieve differentiation means that:

- a company's strategy must rest on unique activities based on customer needs, customer accessibility or the variety of its products or services

- a company's activities must fit and link together – in terms of the value chain, one link is prone to imitation, but with a chain imitation is difficult

- a company must make trade-offs. Excelling at some things means making a conscious decision not to do others – being a 'master of one trade' to stand out from the crowd as opposed to being a 'jack of all trades' and lost in the crowd. Trade-offs purposefully limit what a company offers. The essence of strategy lies in what not to do.

The internet

In 2001 Porter addressed the assertion that the internet rendered strategy obsolete. While admitting that the internet was in its infancy, he observed that relying solely on internet technologies to gain market penetration was already proving not to be a sound approach. In a *Harvard Business Review* article in March 2001, Porter said:

In our quest to see how the internet is different, we have failed to see how the internet is the same.

He argued that many internet companies were competing through unsustainable, artificial means, usually propped up by short-term capital investment. He also argued that while the excitement of the internet appeared to throw up new rules of competition, the first wave of excitement was now clearly over, and the old rules and strategic principles appeared to be re-establishing themselves. He gave examples, such as:

- The right goal – a healthy long-term return on investment.

- Value – a company must offer a set of benefits that set it apart from the competition.

- A company's value chain has to do things differently or do different things from rivals to reflect, produce and deliver that value.

- Trade-offs – make conscious deliberate sacrifices in some areas in order to excel, or even be unique, in others.

- All the different components in the value chain must fit together, reinforcing each other to create uniqueness and value. This is what makes a core competence – something that is difficult to imitate.

- Continuity – not only from a customer perspective but also in order to build and develop skills that provide a competitive edge.

Porter foresaw that as most businesses embraced the internet, it would become nullified as a source of advantage, while traditional strengths such as uniqueness, design and service relationships would re-emerge. For Porter the next phase of internet evolution would be more holistic, with a shift from e-business to business, from e-learning to learning, within which the internet would be a communications medium and not necessarily a source of advantage.

In perspective

It is a mark of Porter's achievement that much of his work on competitive strategy, researched in the 1970s, still has high value and relevance in the 21st century, and still shapes mainstream thinking on competition and strategy.

Although now much quoted, the following was intended to be as much a of a compliment as *The Economist* ('Professor Porter PhD', 8 October 1994) could muster:

His work is academic to a fault … Mr Porter is about as likely to produce a blockbuster full of anecdotes and boosterish catch-phrases as he is to deliver a lecture dressed in bra and stockings.

While his work is academically rigorous, his ability to abstract his thinking into digestible chunks for the business world has given him wide appeal in both the academic and business worlds. It is now standard practice for organisations to think and talk about value chains, and the five forces have entered the curriculum of every management programme. Porter's later thinking on strategy rides the new wave of revolutionary strategic thinking led by Hamel and links consistently with his earlier work. One suspects not only that there is more to come from Porter, but also that it will be wholly consistent with what he has said in the past.

Performing a SWOT analysis

SWOT analysis is a diagnostic tool for strategic planning which involves the identification and evaluation of strengths, weaknesses, opportunities and threats. This framework facilitates the assessment of internal capabilities and resources that are under the control of the organisation and of external factors that are not under organisational control. SWOT analysis involves the collection of information, rather than the framing of recommendations, which can only be considered once the facts have been confirmed. The analysis may be carried out by a single manager, but it usually involves the participation of a wider group, so that insights can be gained from across the organisation or department.

SWOT analysis emerged in the 1960s from research at Stanford Research Institute into the failure of current corporate planning methods. The technique evolved, became widely used during the 1980s and remains popular, although critics have pointed out weaknesses in its application, including a lack of analytical depth. It provides a simple framework for analysing the market position of an organisation and can be applied in a range of planning and strategic contexts including strategy development, marketing planning, and the evaluation of strategic options for a whole business or an individual department. It may be used in conjunction with tools such as PEST (political, economic, social, technological) analysis, or one of its variants, or five forces analysis, which can provide a deeper understanding of the external environment and help to assess potential risks and threats to the profitability and survival of the organisation. SWOT analysis is also used by individuals to assess personal career prospects, but this checklist focuses on its use by organisations and departments and does not cover the individual aspect.

Action checklist

1 Establish the objectives

The first step in any management project is to be clear about what you are doing and why. The purpose of conducting a SWOT analysis may be wide or narrow, general or specific – anything from getting staff to think about and understand the business better, to rethinking a strategy or the overall direction of the business. SWOT analysis usually focuses on the present situation. In the context of scenario planning, however, it could be used to look into the future and, using appreciative inquiry methods, to assess what factors have made the organisation successful in the past.

2 Select appropriate contributors

This is important if the final recommendations are to result from consultation and discussion, not just personal views, however expert. If you are conducting an organisation-wide analysis, it is important to include people from different departments to make sure that information is gathered from across the business:

- Pick a mix of specialist and 'ideas' people with the ability and enthusiasm to contribute.

- Consider including a mix of staff from different grades, if appropriate.

- Think about numbers. Six to ten people may be enough, especially in a SWOT workshop. Up to twenty-five or thirty can be useful if one of the aims is to help staff see the need for change, but it will be necessary to split into smaller groups for the more active parts of the process.

3 Allocate research and information-gathering tasks

Background preparation is vital if the subsequent analysis is to be accurate, and should be divided among the SWOT participants. Preparation can be carried out in two stages: exploratory, followed by data collection; and detailed, followed by a focused analysis.

- Gathering information on strengths and weaknesses should focus on the internal factors of skills, resources and assets, or the lack of them.

- Gathering information on opportunities and threats should focus on the external factors over which you have little or no control, such as social, market or economic trends.

However, you will need to be aware of and take account of the interrelationships between internal and external factors.

4 Create a workshop environment

If the compilation and recording of SWOT lists takes place in meetings, make sure that you exploit the benefits of workshop sessions. Foster an atmosphere conducive to the free flow of information and encourage participants to say what they feel is appropriate, without fearing or attributing blame. The leader or facilitator has a key role and should allow time for thought, but not so much as to let the discussion stagnate. Half an hour is often enough to spend on strengths, for example, before moving on. It is important to be specific, evaluative and analytical at the stage of compiling and recording the SWOT lists – mere description is not enough.

5 List strengths

It is often harder to identify strengths than weaknesses. Questions such as the following can be helpful:

- What do we do better than anyone else?
- What advantages do we have?

- What unique resources do we have?
- What do others see as our strong points?

Strengths may relate to the organisation – its market share, reputation and people, including the skills and knowledge of staff – as well as reasons for past successes. Try to be as specific as possible when collecting facts. For example, it is not sufficient to say that the level of profit is good. If the profit margin is 10% but the industry average is 30%, for example, there is clearly room for improvement.

Other people strengths include:

- friendly, cooperative and supportive staff
- a staff development and training scheme
- appropriate levels of involvement through delegation and trust.

Organisational strengths may include:

- customer loyalty, for example 90% repeat customers
- capital investment and a strong balance sheet, with a higher profit margin than other organisations in the sector
- effective cash management resulting in, say, 25 days' accounts receivable as opposed to a norm of 36 days in the same industry
- efficient procedures and systems showing, for example, a 3% reduction in expenses over the past five years
- well-developed corporate social responsibility policies.

6 List weaknesses

This session should not be seen as an opportunity to criticise the organisation but as an honest appraisal of the way things are. Be careful not to take weaknesses at face value, but to identify the underlying causes.

Key questions include:

- What is hindering progress?
- What needs improving?

- Where are complaints coming from?
- Are there any weak links in the chain?

  The list might include:

- customers looking for more products or services
- declining sales of the main or most popular products or services
- poor competitiveness, as demonstrated by figures showing the percentage of market share lost over the past three years and higher price increases compared with those of competitors
- non-compliance with, or ignorance of, appropriate legislation
- financial or cash flow problems
- employees not aware of the organisation's mission, objectives and policies
- high levels of staff absence compared with average levels in the sector or rising levels of absence
- no processes in place for monitoring success or failure.

  It is not unusual for 'people problems' – poor communication, inadequate leadership, lack of motivation, too little delegation, absence of trust – to feature among the major weaknesses.

7 List opportunities

This step is designed to assess the socio-economic, political, environmental and demographic factors that affect organisational performance. The aim is to identify circumstances that the organisation can exploit and to evaluate their possible benefits.

Examples include:

- technological developments
- new markets
- change of government
- changes in interest rates
- demographic trends

- strengths and weaknesses of competitors.

Bear in mind that opportunities may be time-limited and consider how the organisation may make the most of them.

8 List threats

Threats are the opposite of opportunities. All the factors listed above may, with a shift of emphasis or perception, also have an adverse impact.

The questions to ask include:

- What are our competitors doing?
- What changes are there in the market for our products?
- What resource problems do we have?
- What is the impact of the economy on our bottom line?

Threats may include:

- unemployment levels
- skills shortages
- environmental legislation
- new technologies that will make our products or services obsolete.

It is important to look at a worst-case scenario. However, this should not be allowed to foster pessimism; it is rather a question of assessing risks and considering how potential problems may be limited or eliminated. Most external factors are challenges, and whether staff perceive them as opportunities or threats is often a valuable indicator of morale.

9 Evaluate listed ideas against objectives

With the lists compiled, sort and group facts and ideas in relation to your objectives. Consider which of the factors listed are of major importance and which are negligible. It may be necessary for the SWOT participants to select their five most important items from the list to gain a broad perspective. The key to this process is clarity of objectives, as evaluation and elimination will be necessary to separate the wheat from the chaff. Although some aspects may require further investigation or research, a clear picture should start to emerge at this stage.

10 Carry your findings forward

Once the SWOT analysis is complete, you need to address the question of how the potential of strengths and opportunities can be maximised and how the risks implicit in weaknesses and threats can be minimised. Bear in mind that much of the information you have collected will represent symptoms rather than root causes, so further consideration of the underlying issues may be needed. However good or bad the results of the analysis are, make sure that they are integrated into subsequent planning and strategy development. Revisit the findings at suitable intervals to check that they are still valid.

As a manager you should avoid:

- giving undue weight to opinions which are not based on hard evidence
- ignoring the ideas of participants at lower levels in the organisational hierarchy
- succumbing to 'paralysis by analysis'
- allowing the process to become an exercise in blame laying or a vehicle for criticism and recrimination
- seeing SWOT analysis as an end in itself and failing to integrate the results into subsequent planning.

Carrying out a PEST analysis

PEST analysis is a technique used to identify, assess and evaluate external factors affecting the performance of an organisation with the aim of gathering information to guide strategic decision-making.

PEST analysis is a useful tool for understanding the wider environment in which an organisation operates. It involves reviewing factors which will have an impact on the organisation's business and the level of success it will be able to achieve and may be carried out as part of an ongoing process of environmental scanning, to inform overall strategy development, or to support the development of a new product or service. Undertaking a PEST analysis can raise awareness of threats to profitability and help to anticipate future difficulties, so that action to avoid or minimise their effects can be taken. It can also alert the organisation to promising business opportunities for the future. The process of carrying out the analysis will also help to develop the ability to think strategically.

Traditionally, PEST analysis has focused on political, economic, sociological and technological factors, but increasing awareness of the importance of legal, environmental and cultural factors has led to the evolution of a growing number of variants. For example:

- PESTLE – political, economic, social, technological, legal and environmental
- SPECTACLES – social, political, economic, cultural, technological, aesthetic, customers, legal, environmental, sectoral

- PEST-C – where C stands for cultural
- SLEEPT-C – sociological, legal, economic, environmental, political, technological and cultural.

This checklist focuses on the traditional four-factor analysis, but it is important for managers and business leaders to consider which additional factors are particularly relevant to their organisation and to include these in the analysis.

Framework for the analysis

To facilitate the analysis, it can be helpful to create a matrix of the factors to be analysed and the opportunities or threats they represent, as in the table below. This provides a simple framework for the analysis, but bear in mind that there will be varying degrees of overlap and interrelation between the different factors.

	Opportunities	Threats
Political		
Economic		
Sociological		
Technological		

Political factors

This part of the analysis is concerned with how the policies and actions of government affect the conduct of business. Legislation may restrict or protect commercial operations in a number of ways. Issues to be considered under this heading include:

- the level of political stability
- the legislative and regulatory framework for business, employment and trade
- the tax regime and fiscal policy
- programmes of forthcoming legislation
- the dominant political ideology.

Questions to ask:

- When is the next election due?
- How likely is a change of government?
- Is the government inclined towards interventionist or laissez-faire policies?
- What is the government's approach to issues such as tax, competition, corporate social responsibility and environmental issues?
- How do sector rules and regulations affect your business?

Economic factors

This part of the analysis is concerned with overall prospects for the economy. Key measures include:

- GDP/GNP
- inflation
- interest rates
- exchange rates
- unemployment figures
- wage and price controls
- fiscal and monetary policy.

Issues such as the availability of raw materials and energy resources, the condition of infrastructure and distribution networks, and the changing nature of global competition may also be relevant.

Questions to ask:

- Is the economy in a period of growth, stagnation or recession?
- How stable is the currency?
- Are changes in disposable income to be expected?
- How easily is credit available?

Social factors

These are probably the most difficult factors to quantify and predict, as personal attitudes, values and beliefs are involved. Demographic factors such as birth rates, population growth, regional population shifts, life expectancy or a change in the age distribution of the population should be taken into account. Factors to be considered include:

- levels of education
- employment patterns
- career expectations
- family relationships
- lifestyle preferences
- trends in fashion and taste
- spending patterns
- mobility
- religious beliefs
- consumer activism.

Questions to ask:

- How much leisure time is available to customers?
- How is wealth distributed throughout the population?
- How important are environmental issues?
- What moral or ethical concerns are reflected in the media?
- What might be the impact of an unknown retirement age?

Technological factors

Rapid technological change has had far-reaching effects on business in past decades. Factors to be considered here include:

- investment in research and development
- new technologies and inventions

- internet and e-commerce developments
- developments in production technology
- rates of obsolescence.

Questions to ask:

- Which new technological developments will have implications for my business?
- Where are research and development efforts focused and is there a match with our own focus?
- How are communication and distribution operations being affected by new technologies?

Action checklist

1 Identify the most important issues

The usefulness of the analysis will depend not so much on the quantity of information collected but on its relevance. Consider which factors are most likely to have an impact on the performance of the organisation, taking into account the business it is in and the fields where it is active or may be active in the future. Local and national factors will usually be most important for small businesses, but larger companies will need to consider the environment in any countries in which they do business, as well as the global scene and emergent competition. Information on current and potential changes in the environment should be included.

2 Decide how the information is to be collected and by whom

Check first how much of the required information has already been collected or is available within the organisation in reports, memos and planning documents. In a large organisation, it may be wise to consult those with expertise in specific areas and delegate to them the collection of some types of information.

3 Identify appropriate sources of information

Hard factual information, such as employment figures, inflation and interest rates, and demographics, is often easily available from official statistical sources and reference books. A wide range of additional sources, such as newspapers, magazines, trade journals, research reports, websites, discussion boards, email newsletters and social networking sites, will be needed for softer information such as consumer attitudes and public perceptions. You may also wish to ask consultants, researchers and known experts in the relevant fields to supplement published material.

4 Gather the information

Decide in advance how the information is to be organised and stored, and ensure that the required computer systems for storage and analysis are in place. Take into consideration factors such as the resources available and the personnel who will need to access the information.

5 Analyse the findings

Assess the rate of change in each area: which changes are of minor or major importance, and which are likely to have positive or negative implications. It is possible that some trends will have both positive and negative effects and it will be necessary to weigh these against each other. Avoid overemphasising events with a negative effect and try to identify positive opportunities that may open up. Although a PEST analysis often focuses on anticipating changes in the environment, it is also important to consider areas where little or no change is expected.

6 Identify strategic options

Consider which strategies have the best chances of success and what actions could or should be taken to minimise threats and maximise opportunities.

7 Write a report

Summarise your findings, setting out the threats and opportunities identified and the policy choices that should be considered. Use appendices to include relevant information. Preliminary recommendations for action should also be included.

8 Disseminate your findings

The results of a PEST analysis will be useful to those in the organisation who are responsible for decision-making and strategy formulation.

9 Decide which trends should continue to be monitored

Trends and patterns will emerge from the research and it may be clear that an ongoing review of developments in these areas will be needed. Alternatively, further evidence may be required to support hunches or hypotheses that have been formed during the analysis. Risks will need specific attention and monitoring.

As a manager you should avoid:

● making assumptions about the future based solely on the past or the present – PEST is a diagnostic tool and many other factors should be included before reaching a conclusion

● getting bogged down in collecting vast amounts of detailed information without analysing your findings

● seeing PEST analysis as a one-off – it should form part of an ongoing process for monitoring changes in the business environment

● using PEST analysis in isolation – combine it with other techniques, such as SWOT analysis, Porter's five forces, competitor analysis or scenario planning.

Market analysis: researching new markets

Market analysis is comprehensive marketing research that yields information about the marketplace, including competitors, market size and overall market value. It also reveals trends that can be used to predict the relative growth or decline of a target market.

There are many reasons organisations seek new markets within which to operate. A market may become saturated or overcrowded. Or a market may be in decline with diminishing returns. Competition from a few dominating players may be too strong, effectively eradicating opportunities for others' market share. Or demand for a product or service may have waned, making diversification necessary.

As well as seeking new markets for survival and continued sustainability, organisations are looking for new opportunities in order to grow. Business start-ups and innovators also need to identify and research viable markets in which to launch their fresh offerings.

The urgency of finding a new market and new opportunities varies depending on circumstances. It may be necessary to find a new market quickly in order to capitalise on a time-sensitive product or service. Conversely, you may have the luxury of waiting six months or more before launch. The attractiveness of opportunities varies and timing has a crucial role to play in maximising the potential rewards offered by a new market.

Undertaking detailed market research is essential in order to inform decision-making. Accurate, timely data will put you in the best position to gain an insight into your target sector and to determine whether you have identified the right market, at the right time, for your product or service to prosper.

This checklist provides guidance on researching new markets and covers issues to consider before contemplating market entry.

Action checklist

1 Be clear about the target market

Scope out the market or market segment you wish to investigate. For example, are you seeking:

- a new segment within your existing market
- a new industry
- a different geographical region
- an overseas market?

Also take into account whether you intend to market an established product or service to a new audience, or whether you are launching an entirely new product or service. Determining such criteria at the outset will give you a good starting point from which to begin your research.

2 Research the market and collect the data

Market insights need to be based on well-researched facts, not on vague assumptions or optimism. It is crucial, therefore, to undertake detailed market research in order to gain a sound understanding of the current state of the market.

Devise a strategy for data gathering and collation. Begin by determining what you want to find out and how you will go about finding it.

There are two types of information sources:

- **Primary** – information gained directly from individual sources, i.e. your target customers. Methods of acquiring primary data include interviews, surveys, questionnaires and focus groups. Decide who will be selected for your sample and how they will be contacted.

- **Secondary** – information that has been gathered by a third party and is readily available to consult. Secondary information is located in various places such as industry and sector reports, government reports, news reports, census data, company databases and the internet.

Consider the time, cost and resource implications before selecting your chosen methods. Also establish which sources will provide the most current and factual account of the market. Different approaches have their advantages and disadvantages, so think about how best to provide the answers you are seeking. Select your data gathering method: qualitative or quantitative (or both). Base your decision on what you want to find out and how the findings will be presented to others.

Remember that the business environment can change rapidly, so make certain that the information used to inform decision-making is accurate, current and valid. Also ensure that the information you gather is from a reliable, trusted source to increase the credibility and value of your facts.

3 Use existing networks and build new ones

Vital market information can also be acquired from an established network of industry experts. So look to your network to increase your knowledge of the current marketplace. If your new target market is similar to the one in which you currently operate, your existing contacts may provide useful insights into the market. Conversely, it may be necessary to establish new industry contacts to satisfy your knowledge needs. Take the time to identify key people in the appropriate fields and gradually build up a network of trusted people.

As well as helping you to learn about your new market through 'insider' knowledge, establishing relationships with industry experts at this stage will also help strengthen your position should you decide to enter this new market in the future.

4 Communicate with your customers

The development of social media networks has opened up opportunities for organisations to interact with customers and potential customers, and valuable intelligence can be gained in this way. Use your relationship with existing customers to find out what is not being provided by you or the wider marketplace. By talking candidly, you may discover opportunities to diversify into new markets to satisfy unmet needs or demand.

5 Keep track of what your competitors are doing

As well as your customers, you could also benefit from looking at the practices and growth strategies of your competitors. See whether they are diversifying their offering and whether this is helping them to enter new markets. If others have identified potential opportunities in different markets, consider whether you could be successful there too.

6 Analyse market trends

In times of rapid change, it has become increasingly difficult to produce credible forecasts. Nonetheless, it is still worth looking at past and current trends in your target market. Use the data you have gathered to help predict whether a market is likely to grow, plateau or decline and determine whether the trends indicate a change in customers' current and future buying habits.

Market trends can be categorised in the following ways:

- **Demographic** – changing population patterns in different demographic groups such as age and ethnicity.
- **Economic** – fluctuations in the economy such as interest levels, personal income, taxation, etc.
- **Sociocultural** – trends in lifestyle activities and choices.
- **Natural** – trends in the changing natural environment, such as global warming, increasing scarcity of natural fuels, etc.
- **Technological** – trends in this arena change rapidly, with

advances in technology having a far-reaching impact on numerous products, services and operations.

- **Regulatory** – changes to legislation and regulations.

Political changes and political stability can have a bearing on current and future demand for products and services. Use such trends to help predict buyer behaviour. Consider the trending areas and determine what impact they could have in the future. To what extent have they affected the market already?

7 Determine market size

To assess a market's relative attractiveness and its potential to offer the opportunities you are seeking, you will need to calculate the overall market size and its current value. An estimation of current market size can be made by calculating:

- the number of customers or businesses it currently serves
- the aggregate spend by those customers
- the number of units being sold.

As well as determining the size of the current market, calculate what percentage of the market share you need to command to sustain or grow your business. A market may be large, but it may not be an attractive proposition if it is already filled with too many competing companies. Similarly, a smaller market may offer less growth in the long term but is also less likely to attract large competitors. Weigh up the pros and cons of each and decide what size of market fits your ambitions.

8 Evaluate growth potential

As well as calculating the size of the market, you also need to estimate its potential for growth over the long term. Use the current and future trending data you have compiled as a means of predicting the potential for the market to expand. Take heed of negative trends, as you do not want to be targeting a market that is already saturated and/or is showing signs of decline.

Compare the performance of the market as it stands today with its position 1–5 years ago. This should indicate a clear trend towards either growth or decline. If your market shows inconsistent performance over a five-year period, decide whether you think the level of risk is acceptable. If your target market shows signs of having reached a plateau, consider whether future forecasts indicate it is likely to increase in the coming years or whether the market has become exhausted and will naturally decline.

Remember that a market can grow rapidly only to plateau or decline shortly afterwards once demand has been satisfied. Determine whether your target market offers only a short-term advantage or has the capacity for prolonged growth.

9 Research the competition

If you have established that your target market is large enough to accommodate another entrant and is trending towards continued and sustained future growth, you may decide that it is an attractive proposition. However, when considering a new market you also need to take into account the players already operating within it. The pool of potential customers may be large, but the level of competition may be high.

Find out who your potential competitors are – both direct and indirect – and what percentage of the market they currently command:

- How many are there?
- Who are the market leaders?
- What threats do they pose?
- Do current players in the market allow 'room' for you to make your presence felt?
- Or is the market dominated by one or two companies which have commandeered the lion's share?

Examine your positioning strategy and the differentiation that will set you apart from the competition. Porter's five forces model may be a useful tool for considering your competitive position within a new market. The five identified forces can be used to determine the relative attractiveness of the market and whether you can successfully compete within it.

Consider the impact of the following:

- entry into the market of new competitors
- the threat of substitutes offering cheaper alternatives
- the bargaining power of buyers or customers
- the bargaining power of suppliers
- the level of competition from existing competitors.

Assess your own organisation's position and rate each of the forces as favourable or unfavourable to determine how acceptable the target market actually is.

10 Identify new market threats

As well as competitors, identify all other perceived risks or threats posed by the new market. Your chances of success in a competitive marketplace will be threatened if:

- the market is fairly static, with little room for growth
- costs are fixed
- your product differentiation is low
- economies of scale are low
- competitor rivalry is fierce, e.g. competitors are undercutting each other in order to secure custom
- you lack the required skills and knowledge to compete
- you lack the required resources in terms of staffing, time and finances.

Contemplate the implications of potential risks and decide how these can be minimised. Risks may be overcome simply by making adjustments to your current operations, or by delaying the time of entry to a more opportune moment. Conversely, you may decide that the risks are simply too great.

11 Analyse the data and report your findings

Once all the information has been gathered and collated, the findings need to be carefully analysed, with rational conclusions drawn. The data will inform decision-making, so it is important to spend the time and effort needed to interpret the information. Remember to focus on the facts as they are presented – not what you want them to show. Although the findings may well reaffirm previously held assumptions about your target market, they could equally reveal something that you had not foreseen.

Adopt a consistent approach to recording and interpreting information so that it can be easily understood by others in the organisation. Devise a means of reporting the findings to senior management and other interested parties and arrange a time and date to present the information to them. Draw attention to the key findings revealed by your research and highlight the action points raised. Use the evidence to reach viable conclusions and support recommendations. Decide what the points of action will be and assign responsibility to see them through.

The findings of your market research are a valuable asset to your organisation, so be wary of distributing the results to external personnel.

12 Consider targeting a segment of a new market

Targeting a segment of a proposed market may be an attractive proposition to start-ups or small businesses seeking to begin operating on a small scale or targeting a niche set of customers. Although it is unlikely that capturing a segment of the market alone will be enough to grow a business or sustain it in the long term, it may be something you wish to consider if the business is young and looking to grow slowly. This can effectively keep you out of the eye-line of larger competitors, allowing you to develop reasonably undetected by your rivals. Once you have established a foothold, you may then be in a stronger position to compete in the overall market with the established players.

Determine the size of the segment and how fast it is growing (or declining). If you wish to expand your business in the future, find out whether the segment you are initially targeting will effectively provide entry into other market segments at a later stage.

13 Beware of being first to market

Be aware of the risks of targeting a new or newly emerging market. The first entrant to a market rarely ends up dominating it in the long term. Indeed, early entrants often expend time and effort building up an interest in the market only to be trumped by later entrants who capitalise on their hard work. So consider whether waiting for the market to become established will be more profitable for you in the long term.

14 Realise your return on investment

The time and costs involved in entering a new market are considerable. Typically, it takes 5–7 years before the prospects of a new investment are fully realised. You need to be confident that the market you have identified has the longevity to enable you to realise a return and that you will be able to gain sufficient market share to operate comfortably alongside your competitors.

As a manager you should avoid:

- failing to carry out thorough market research
- targeting a declining market
- dismissing unfavourable trends
- ignoring new market threats
- being first to market.

Using scenarios

Scenarios are a projection of possible or imagined sequences of future events. They can be broad-ranging and contradictory. However, scenarios are not forecasts. They describe a series of events or changes that could happen, as opposed to asserting that something will happen. They are generally presented as stories formed around plots, highlighting the significant components of the future. Scenario planning involves elements of intuition as well as analytical approaches to gathering information and data.

Scenario planning is a set of processes for describing and evaluating scenarios. It helps business leaders to understand different possible futures and the internal and external factors that drive them, and to test strategies for dealing with these potential futures.

Successfully adapting to change is fundamental for a company's continued growth and survival. To retain competitive advantage in an ever-evolving marketplace, organisations need to keep one step ahead of the competition. Regardless of whether change is predictable or unforeseen, it nevertheless should be planned for. Even planning for a known future is difficult, but how can you prepare your organisation for a future that is completely unknown? Answer: by using what is known and applying it in the creation of scenarios. Scenarios help managers prepare for the future by encouraging them to ask a series of what-if questions, considering several possible futures that may have a significant impact upon their organisation. This prepares them for eventualities before they actually happen. In this respect, scenarios complement more traditional forms of business planning and act as a form of contingency planning. Potential future break points in the marketplace that will affect the business are identified and response strategies can be prepared in advance.

Opinions differ as to the order of steps in the process of scenario planning and the weight to be given to each. The following checklist provides a general framework for developing and analysing scenarios.

Action checklist

1 Set objectives

To provide a sound structure for each scenario, set a framework of clear objectives. All parties involved in the creation of scenarios should agree on this process.

Ask questions such as:

- Where do we want to be in the future?
- What will it take to get us there?
- How long will it take?
- What could hinder us?
- What issues have caused us problems in the past?
- What do we want to avoid?
- How will we measure our achievement?

Pointers to consider include the following:

- **Time projection** – set a short- or long-term time horizon for each scenario.
- **Business area coverage** – scenarios can be projected futures of the organisation in its entirety or can focus upon specific areas or products.

- **Geographical coverage** – for multi-site and global organisations, consider whether the scenarios are relevant in each location (for example, economic and political changes may affect only one geographical area).

- **Team building** – establish a team of managers who will be responsible for designing each scenario.

- **Set a deadline** – agree a time limit when building the scenarios.

- **Measures** – where appropriate, set measures of performance that will help to monitor the achievement of your objectives.

2 Work as a team

Traditionally, the creation of scenarios has been the responsibility of senior managers, as they have the ultimate responsibility for a business's strategic decisions. However, managers at all levels of the organisation need to participate in the scenario-building exercise to ensure that their knowledge, insight and ideas are shared. Conducting interviews and holding discussions with key players will foster communication and knowledge transfer across the whole team. A scenario should be engaging and challenging, so encourage the management team to be creative in their projections of the future.

3 Gather information on trends and factors

Managers should use the known to plan for the unknown. For example, the arrival of a new competitor may be known, but the full details of its operation may not be. It is known that they are a threat, but the extent of the threat is unknown. So in this example, managers can form a scenario based upon the known facts and then hypothesise the impact as part of the scenario planning process. By utilising existing knowledge, managers will be able to propose realistic future projections, which in turn can be used to create effective scenarios for coping with the unexpected. Although it is important to encourage creative thinking, scenarios should nevertheless be realistic. To achieve this, managers must have a sound understanding of the facts to ensure that the scenarios can help to guide practical business decisions.

Where possible, gather information from inside and outside the organisation to fill any knowledge gaps. You may wish to use techniques such as PEST analysis or one of its variants to assess the business environment and identify important factors that will affect the organisation. At this stage, it is important to be clear about the different types of information that will form the basis of the scenarios.

These include:

- factual data on historical trends
- informed opinion – the views of experts
- values and norms – the beliefs and perceptions of individuals and groups
- concepts – radical new ideas about the future.

4 Challenge assumptions

Inevitably, elements of disagreement within the scenario team will arise as each member presents their opinion on the impact a driver of change may have upon the organisation's future. Therefore be prepared to challenge previously held theories. Consider the assumptions that support each plot as a means of finding a common agreed projection of the future. The perceptions of individual managers may be limited to the impact a change agent has on areas of direct concern to themselves. Thus it is imperative for this group exercise to elicit a range of conceivable outcomes so as to create the most plausible scenarios that can be applied to the wider organisation.

5 Consider the future

Once the objectives of each scenario have been established, the next step in ensuring the creation of plausible scenarios is to pose a series of what-if questions with related dilemmas. Consider different possible futures and decide what actions would need to be taken to cope effectively with unpredictable change. Ask largely open-ended questions to explore the wide range of possible futures. In particular, examine the main threats to the organisation together with their related consequences:

- **change drivers** – technology, economy, politics
- **impact** – the level of impact each driver will have
- **likelihood** – how likely it is that such a driver will occur
- **uncertainties** – unknown elements that can be grouped together to form the basis of credible scenarios.

The creation of scenarios will take time to perfect, but, when done correctly, it is nevertheless an effective tool for imagining futures. Therefore, it is worth taking time and effort to consider carefully which scenarios are worth developing further.

6 Build the scenarios

Scenarios are typically presented as stories, but they can also take the form of scripts or timelines. To create a scenario in response to the set of what-if questions, four interrelated scenario elements need to be developed:

- **End-state** – the state of the world at the end of the scenario period, i.e. what the future marketplace might look like.

- **Plot** – provides details of what would have to happen for the end-state to occur.

- **Driving forces** – these shape plots; the events, the decisions and actions that would cause the plot to evolve in a particular way.

- **Logic** – provides a rationale for why a particular plot and associated end-state would unfold.

Sufficient scenarios should be developed to cover probable and possible futures and related impacts. However, avoid designing too many scenarios, as this will just lead to confusion. Four scenarios is the recommended maximum. Elements to consider in scenario formulation include:

- **description** – develop detailed and engaging descriptions of the scenarios

- **evidence** – formulate scenarios based upon research and analysis to make them credible
- **effect** – consider the impact scenarios will have upon the organisation
- **warning** – identify early indicators of change
- **usage** – consider how the scenarios will be used.

7 Analyse the scenarios

Scenarios provide vantage points from which to re-examine how the marketplace is functioning, which driving forces are precipitating change and why change might take one particular direction rather than another. They may highlight previously unexpected elements of the future. It is important, therefore, to examine them in order to identify key turning points and market discontinuities that would have a significant impact on the organisation.

8 Examine current policies and strategy

The development of scenarios is pointless unless the implications for current organisational policies and strategies are considered. Examine current strategies to assess whether they will be able to cope with potential changes and turning points. It may be necessary to modify and adapt current strategy in the light of what has been learned. Response strategies for potential futures should be developed, bearing in mind that the future is never certain and strategies will need to be flexible enough to be adapted to unexpected changes. For relatively unlikely scenarios, these strategies may be seen as contingency measures.

9 Evaluate and review

Change is constant and ever-evolving, so to ensure that scenarios remain relevant and credible they need to be regularly reviewed, evaluated and updated as necessary in line with changes to market forces. An out-of-date scenario will be ineffective in preparing an organisation for a sudden change in market conditions. Setting out a clear policy ensures that each scenario is regularly amended and thus remains effective as a coping strategy in the event of significant change.

Considerations to be addressed include:

- how the process is to be monitored
- strict deadlines for reviewing and amending scenarios
- allocation of responsibility for reviewing to a member, or members, of the scenario team
- how the implications for each scenario will be assessed when change occurs.

10 Utilise scenarios throughout the organisation

Once a credible scenario has been formulated, it can be utilised in a variety of different contexts such as HR planning, market research, product development and risk assessment. By considering alternative futures and assessing their relative impacts upon an organisation, scenarios can be used to challenge existing business plans and inspire new ideas. With the presentation of a range of alternative futures, the business plan can become more flexible as it adapts to the ever-evolving business environment.

As a manager you should avoid:

- viewing scenario planning as a one-off exercise
- limiting the number of what-if questions asked
- relying on one scenario which could limit a company's strategic thinking
- seeing scenarios as firm forecasts of the future
- relying exclusively on the insight of senior managers
- developing a confusing number of multiple scenarios.

Strategic risk management

Risk management is the discipline of continuously analysing and assessing the internal and external risks to which an organisation is exposed, both actual and potential, with a view to strengthening strategic decision-making capabilities and planning contingencies.

High-profile failures of risk management in recent years have made it a topic of everyday conversations and political discussions. The collapses of investment banks Bear Stearns and Lehman Brothers in 2008, and the fatal fire and consequent ecological disaster at BP's Deepwater Horizon oil platform in the Gulf of Mexico in 2010, made headline news around the world and prompted calls for regulatory responses.

Intellectually, there has been a rapid popularisation of some relatively new concepts. A better understanding of how human cognitive biases can skew priorities and distract people from emerging risks, even among the most highly qualified and rationally minded senior teams, has deepened our collective awareness. Also influential has been the 'Black Swan' concept, popularised by Nassim Nicholas Taleb, a former financial markets trader and one of the few individuals who warned of the inherent risk in investment banks' market-modelling before the 2008 crash. He emphasises that major external threats can arise suddenly without warning and that, as with many activities which involve human behaviour, it is impossible to create reliable models of markets.

These factors have prompted much rethinking around strategic risk management. There is a movement away from treating risk management as a single specialism, and a realisation that it is unwise to rely exclusively on checklists, regulations or quantitative information to manage organisational risks. Risk must be understood and considered across the management team. Risk management must involve multidisciplinary, in-depth discussions and scenario planning, and be closely linked to strategy development. Some business leaders adopt a yet more radical approach, reconceptualising strategic risk management as a source of competitive advantage, rather than a necessary evil.

Although checklists and procedures should not be the only tools for risk management, they can be useful resources, especially at an operational level. Important examples include procedures for handling hazardous substances, preventing occupational illnesses or minimising the risk of fraud.

It is wise for managers at all levels to have good risk awareness, as this can inform career choices as well as operational and strategic decisions.

This checklist is designed to help managers think about the broader strategic elements of managing risk.

Action checklist

1 Develop a behavioural understanding of the business

It is now well understood that excellent recruitment and people management practice provides the best mitigation against internal risks, especially where high-risk posts are concerned. High standards of leadership and communication throughout the business underpin good risk management. Reliance on checklists and regulations is at best of limited value and at worst counterproductive, partly because rules cannot anticipate every scenario, and also because a climate of fear and unthinking adherence to rules can themselves be risky.

2 Distinguish between different types of risk

It is helpful to distinguish between three different categories of risk:

- **internal, preventable risks** relating to performance and conduct
- **calculated strategic risks** such as investment in new markets
- **external risks** including unexpected events such as the Fukushima earthquake and tsunami in 2011, which had a huge impact on Japanese businesses.

Linked to this analysis, many managers find the four Ts – tolerate, treat, transfer or terminate – useful in deciding how to handle risk:

- A decision to **tolerate** risk might be made with regard to an uncertain political situation in a target market, for example.
- In the case of a clear internally generated risk, measures to **treat** the risk would be more appropriate.
- In some cases risk can be **transferred** by outsourcing a function to a specialist external provider with better back-up and specialist skills.
- In other cases, it would be deemed wise to **terminate** risk by, for example, exiting a market where the risks have begun to outweigh the anticipated gains.

3 Assess impact as well as likelihood

The collapse of Lehman Brothers and the explosion of the Deepwater Horizon oil platform could be categorised as low-probability/high-impact events. In the case of collateralised debt obligation trading by investment banks, however, it could be argued that the risk was much higher than analysts believed – a case of overconfidence and confirmation biases. Some useful approaches have been developed to help management teams analyse and understand risks according to both their impact and their likelihood.

Companies are advised to take a strategic view of their own approach to risk, or risk appetite, as it is often called. This should cover matters such as tolerance for debt or strategic approach to acquisitions.

4 Develop a behavioural understanding of markets

Market models based on the probabilities of games of chance where there are known and finite numbers of variables have been challenged by Taleb, who has argued that real markets are different in nature. Much of this behavioural understanding has already been used to inform investments on the financial markets, but the same principles apply to other types of markets. They are made up of human beings making economic decisions, sometimes individually, sometimes as a group, and can be influenced by unpredictable social or meteorological events.

5 Distinguish between risk and uncertainty

The difference between risk (which is identifiable) and uncertainty (which is unforeseen and unpredictable in scale) was usefully defined by Frank Knight, an early 20th-century economist. Traditional assessment tools such as SWOT (strengths, weaknesses, opportunities, threats) and PESTLE (political, economic, social, technological, legal, environmental) can also be used. Some managers also define peripheral risk that may grow in likelihood or potential impact as a 'weak signal' that should be taken into account.

6 Understand cognitive biases

It is well understood that humans as individuals and in groups can be prone to major errors of judgement explained by ingrained cognitive biases. One example is overconfidence bias, which probably explains why so many corporate mergers fail to achieve their expected gains. Another is confirmation bias, in which people pay more attention to evidence that supports their view than to evidence that contradicts it.

7 Build meetings structures that interrogate ideas

Given the nature of cognitive biases, it is generally risky to allow an individual or a small group to make major decisions without their ideas being tested. Many companies have established effective approaches to discuss and assess risks and to debate these thoroughly, with inquirers given licence to play devil's advocate. The principle of individual accountability is important here.

8 Integrate analysis and decision-making, but beware of risk managers 'going native'

Experience shows that while the principles of risk management can be set out quite clearly, it is difficult to maintain operational discipline. Risk assessment needs to be sufficiently close to the business to ensure a good understanding, but not so close that individual risk managers are 'captured' by a local team that is too risk-hungry or, conversely, too risk-averse.

The best organisational approach may depend on the business context. The three major approaches involve the use of independent experts, facilitators, or embedded experts.

9 Build capacity in scenario planning

Scenario planning was developed by Shell, an oil company, in the 1960s. It was one of the few major companies to have envisaged a transition from the old Soviet Union to a more democratic group of countries and freer markets. Before 1989, this was seen by many as less likely than either nuclear war or an expansion of the Soviet empire. As a result, Shell was better placed than many companies for the opening of markets in Eastern Europe in the 1990s. Scenario planning has been used to great effect by many strategic teams, often in conjunction with models to assess the likelihood and impact of likely or potential events.

10 Use good risk management as a source of competitive advantage

Businesses have varying levels of risk appetite with regard to strategic decisions, but all organisations can improve their adaptability and resilience by following the principles outlined above. This can lead to risk management becoming a source of competitive advantage, as it helps organisations to respond to emerging threats and opportunities at a strategic level. Being a resilient organisation can result in enhanced brand image, stronger negotiating positions and many other business advantages.

As a manager you should avoid:

- overreliance on procedures or checklists to prevent accidents
- reliance on legislation relating to risk management
- striving to control everything
- discounting low-probability/high-impact events
- managing for the most easily envisaged risk, rather than the most likely.

Producing a corporate mission

A corporate mission statement is a short, memorable statement that clarifies the reasons for the existence of an organisation and expresses what its purpose is. There is a fine but distinct line between a mission statement and a vision statement, which gives a broad, inspirational image of the future an organisation is aiming to achieve.

For the purposes of this checklist a corporate mission is taken to mean a description of the underpinning purpose of an organisation. A mission statement defines the essence of an organisation and what it stands for. It describes the purpose of the organisation and identifies how the organisation defines success.

The corporate mission may be known as a corporate philosophy or credo. Whatever it is called, it should combine the inspiration of 'where we are going' with the realities of 'where we are now' and 'how we are going to get there'.

The production of an effective mission statement can:

- clarify the role of the organisation in society
- create a central reference point for the development of appropriate goals, targets and strategy
- give stakeholders a clear picture of what the organisation stands for
- help employees understand the nature of the organisation they are working for

- provide a sense of identity, meaning and purpose throughout the organisation.

However, mission statements have been widely criticised as often not being worth the paper they are written on, so it is important to understand that they need to be:

- aligned with organisational vision and values
- incorporated into strategy and practice
- communicated in such a way as to inspire engagement, commitment and buy-in from all employees.

Developing a sense of mission requires strategic thinking, effective internal communication, empowerment and, in some cases, cultural change. This checklist is intended to provide guidance for senior managers who wish to produce a mission statement and develop a sense of mission within their organisation.

Action checklist

1 Create a project team

The senior management team is usually responsible for establishing an organisation's mission, so the project team should consist of either the complete senior management team, or perhaps, in a larger organisation, a working group selected from the senior management team. The process of producing a corporate mission involves an analysis of the strategy and future of the company. Conducting a SWOT analysis of the organisation and its markets can be a helpful start in identifying its strengths and opportunities. The appointment of an external facilitator may help the team if there are likely to be problems in reaching a consensus agreement on the mission.

2 Gather information

The project team should investigate, appraise and define the current ethos and values of the organisation, using internal and external sources or information. Meetings and interviews with senior managers will form part of this process. Other areas to examine should include published and visual materials, the website, the general corporate image or brand and current strategy. Gerry Johnson and Kevan Scholes's model of the 'cultural web' may be helpful here. With a number of influential managers, identify:

- areas of agreement
- conflicts in attitudes
- opinions and strategic thinking
- internal views of the organisation.

External opinion can be researched by means of press files, analysts' reports and the views of customers and suppliers.

When sufficient information has been gathered on internal and external views, they should be reviewed and compared to build a broad picture of the organisation. The project team should collate this information and prepare a detailed report to facilitate the production of the corporate mission statement. As the values are attitudes these will need to be communicated to and accepted by employees.

3 Build consensus

The senior management team needs to reach a consensus on a clear mission for the organisation. This is where an external facilitator can play an important role. The mission should help to define direction, and give a clear declaration of where the management team wants to take the organisation. It should give all stakeholders a clear message on organisational intentions.

Barriers to the adopted direction should be explored and appropriate steps and responsibilities should be agreed for dealing with these obstacles. Resourcing, core organisation competencies and possible employee development needs are among the factors to consider. This process will help the team develop ownership of the mission and take responsibility for it.

4 Draft a mission statement

The mission statement should be written and agreed by the senior management team as a whole, as it needs to draw upon and represent the consensus reached on the future of the organisation. The mission statement acts as the guide for the organisation-wide evolution of a sense of corporate mission.

The following are past and current examples of mission statements from some leading companies:

- **Google** 'to organise the world's information and make it universally accessible and useful'

- **eBay** 'to provide a global trading platform where practically anyone can trade practically anything'

- **Apple** 'to bring the best personal computing experience to students, educators, creative professionals and consumers around the world through its innovative hardware, software and internet offerings'

- **Starbucks** 'to inspire and nurture the human spirit – one person, one cup and one neighborhood at a time'.

Assess (and ask others to assess) the mission statement for clarity, succinctness, memorability, believability and motivational aspects, then revise it as necessary. Bear in mind that a mission statement does not, in itself, create a sense of mission. Employees will respond to a mission statement only if they can understand it, relate to it and own it, so make sure that the wording is clear and simple.

5 Communicate the mission throughout the organisation

Consider how the mission will be communicated throughout the organisation. The range of 'pick and mix' options that can be used includes workshops, cascaded briefings, internal newsletters or bulletins, the intranet or group meetings. It is essential to develop a sense of ownership of the mission throughout the organisation, as only employees can bring the mission to life in their daily activities and dealings with customers.

6 Develop action plans and set objectives

Organisational objectives and strategy define what the organisation needs to do and the approach it will take to fulfil its mission. Action plans can build on the consensus and commitment developed within the senior management team. Set objectives by asking what needs to be done to realise the mission, and plan to overcome major barriers to achieving the vision. This is where the mission process meets with strategy and planning.

7 Monitor and review

The development of a sense of mission is a long-term process. Introduce means of monitoring the views of stakeholders to give indications of the spread of the sense of mission, the relevance of the statement, how well it is understood, and the degree to which corporate values have been cascaded throughout the organisation. Build references and links to the mission statement and values into all organisational activities, meetings and individual performance management practices. Use regular group meetings to promote and develop the philosophy.

8 Use the mission statement to focus the organisation

Developing a sense of mission is usually more successful if it is viewed as a long-term, evolutionary process. Some organisations develop a mission statement that they then use to provide a focus for the business. This approach can be useful, but is usually successful only where there has been close consultation with managers in the development of the mission.

As a manager you should avoid:

● moving forward without a full consensus among the senior team

● neglecting to communicate the mission statement to employees

● forgetting to refer back to the statement and plan in practice.

Corporate values

In *The Nature of Human Values* (1973), Milton Rokeach defines values as 'an enduring belief that a specific mode of conduct or end-state existence is personally or socially preferable to an opposite or converse mode of conduct or end-state existence'. In everyday terms this means that values are our ideas about how things should be; they are the product of the things that we both prefer and prioritise above other things.

Individuals have priority values, as do organisations. The choice is not whether or not to have values – it is whether or not to deliberately work with them.

In starting to think about corporate values try to distinguish between two main types:

- **Core values** are distinctive, deeply ingrained and govern all an organisation's actions. They articulate what fundamentally matters to an organisation. They are a key driver of strategic purpose alongside the vision and the mission.

- **Aspirational values** are values that people may think will be needed to succeed in the future but may not yet be embedded in practice.

Successful organisations are linked with strong values and culture. Values are a key component of an organisation's culture and should underpin the whole organisation by guiding behaviours to support cultural change. Organisations that commit to consciously values-based cultures can drive improvements in productivity and customer satisfaction and achieve long-term competitive advantage. When core values are both effectively expressed and genuinely lived out staff engagement is positively affected, as employees gain a greater sense of meaning in work, which in turn increases motivation and commitment. For corporate values to be meaningful they have to be expressed in terms that make sense to employees. For corporate values to be credible they should align with the strategic purpose of the organisation and be reflected in leadership and management practice.

Formally adopting core values in an organisation is not a quick fix. It takes time and planning to analyse and develop consistent and enduring values, and then to implement them as part of an overall strategy. Core values programmes may encounter problems. Some individuals may feel unsettled by a values initiative if they sense that their own values do not completely align with the corporate values being expressed. Value statements can prompt criticism of managers and leaders who do not appear to be living up to the sentiments expressed. Corporate statements of any kind are useless unless lived out in practice.

When executed well, values programmes make a significant positive difference to attitudes and behaviours at individual and team levels – aspects of organisational life that can be hard to influence through policy or training interventions. Values-congruent organisations enjoy high levels of stakeholder confidence and are often more successful at attracting inward investment than their peers.

Corporate value statements are often used in association with vision, mission and/or purpose statements.

This checklist explores ways to analyse, develop and implement values as part of an overall organisational strategy.

Action checklist

1 Analyse the current situation

Be clear about why your organisation intends to embark upon a values programme and start thinking about how you will measure the progress of the work. You might want to build up basic information on how employees and customers perceive the values expressed by the organisation and how these show up in their behaviour. Review any articles or documents written about the organisation. Which ones express the best characteristics of the organisation? In customer feedback surveys and correspondence, what makes your organisation one that people think well of? Unprompted comments are the best.

You could also use results from performance reviews and/or exit interviews. Focus groups and interviews are useful to delve deeper and find out more. Share all findings, the good and the less good, with the team chosen to work on the values programme.

2 Build the values team

A small team comprising key employees and the chief executive often works most effectively when developing values. Making sure there is visible ownership of the initiative across the whole organisation, rather than just handing it over to the HR department, helps establish credibility and confidence. It is crucial to set the scene and get senior managers to drive and fully support the values process. Ideally, members of the values team should have willingly agreed to take part as opposed to being directed.

3 Identify and articulate core values

There is no ideal number of core values to have: 3–5 is fairly common. The more you have the harder it is for people to remember them and bring them to life in everyday practice.

Your core values should express what is distinct and specific about how your organisation does what it does. Core values need to be more than a simple list of words. Each value should be a word or short phrase with an associated explanation. If you do not state what your organisation means when it says 'trust' or 'excellence' or 'passion', people will draw their own conclusions and the way in which values are transmitted and lived will vary widely. Having a value label – such as trust – followed by a descriptor helps ensure values are meaningful and differentiate your organisation from its competitors. Ask yourself whether the values are easy to understand. Are they memorable? Are they useful in guiding employees to make effective decisions for themselves? Values and values statements need to be long-lasting, so take your time and do not rush their development.

There is no right way to arrive at the core values for your organisation. Some organisations bring in external specialists at this stage, and an objective viewpoint may be useful. Organisational values is a specialist field, so check whether the consultant(s) you are considering have successfully executed similar programmes elsewhere. Employee and stakeholder engagement may be appropriate, but leaders and managers must align with the final iteration of the values and be able to consistently model the values in practice.

4 Assess current strategy in relation to values

Consider how your strategic aims and objectives align with the values. If you are planning changes to your strategy, look at the values and determine how to express those changes in the context of the core values. If values are truly core, they do not change every time there is a new corporate plan or horizon scan.

5 Embed the values into everyday behaviour

There needs to be a correlation between the value statements – what you say you will do – and behaviour – what you actually do and practise daily. The behaviour exhibited has to align with the values.

Reinforce the values and desired behaviour throughout the organisation. During recruitment, for example, provide clear guidance on what the organisation stands for. At interviews, ask questions designed to test alignment or fit with corporate values and recruit people who align with your organisation's values. Embed values in all HR processes including performance management, promotion, pay, rewards and recognition programmes, and disciplinary and dismissal procedures. Recognise employees when they honour the values, and coach or discipline, depending on the situation, employees who do not.

6 Provide meaningful measures

Inspire and engage employees by being transparent about how the organisation is performing. Use a simple scorecard to share performance data, aligning values and behaviour to particular measures. This acts as a reminder that desired behaviour can change and improve scores and have an effect on the bottom line.

7 Communicate the values at every opportunity

Values need to be understood and remembered throughout the organisation. Senior managers should communicate the values and repeat the messages regularly. Stories are a powerful way of communicating values; deliberately collect, share and repeat stories of positive behaviour from employees which demonstrate the values in action. Make sure the values are visible by displaying them on posters, banners, screensavers and even t-shirts and mugs.

8 Live the values

Leaders throughout the organisation should act as role models and live the values by demonstrating desired behaviours. Strategic decisions, for example, can and should be guided by a commitment to the core values. Leaders and managers should be aware of the negative impact dishonouring the corporate values can have on the success of a values initiative.

9 Sustain a values-based culture

Continuous improvement and discipline in embedding the values are crucial to sustaining the values culture, as is making sure that employees are aware that the values adopted represent a permanent change in the organisation.

A yearly review of the progress made in integrating the values into everyday practices is recommended. This can be undertaken by the values team and may result in the implementation of action points and goals to drive improvement.

As a manager you should avoid:

● moving forward without full commitment from the senior management team

● underestimating the time and planning required to develop engaging value statements

● allowing a statement of values to be just a piece of paper

● adopting bland and indistinct values

● failing to communicate the corporate values to employees.

Igor Ansoff
Father of corporate strategy

Introduction

Igor Ansoff (1918–2002) was the originator of the strategic management concept, and was responsible for establishing strategic planning as a management activity in its own right. His landmark book, *Corporate Strategy* (1965), was the first to concentrate entirely on strategy, and although the ideas outlined are complex, it remains one of the classics of management literature.

Life and career

Ansoff was born in Russia and his family emigrated to the US in 1936. His early academic focus was on mathematics, and he obtained a PhD in applied mathematics from Brown University, Rhode Island. He joined the Rand Corporation in 1950, and moved on to Lockheed Aircraft Corporation, where he eventually became vice-president, plans and programmes, and then vice-president and general manager of the industrial technology division.

In 1963, Ansoff was appointed professor of industrial administration at the Carnegie Institute of Technology in Pittsburgh. He went on to hold a number of positions in universities in both the US and Europe. He continued to act as a consultant after retiring from academia in 2000 and, on his retirement, was named Distinguished Professor Emeritus at the United States International University.

Key theories

Until the publication of *Corporate Strategy*, companies had little guidance on how to plan for, or make decisions about, the future. Traditional methods of planning were based on an extended budgeting system using the annual budget, projecting it a few years into the future. By its nature, this system paid little or no attention to strategic issues. However, increasing competition, interest in acquisitions, mergers and diversification and turbulence in the business environment meant that strategic issues could no longer be ignored. Ansoff felt that, in developing strategy, it was essential to systematically anticipate future environmental challenges to an organisation and draw up appropriate strategic plans for responding to these challenges.

In *Corporate Strategy* Ansoff explored these issues, building up a systematic approach to strategy formulation and strategic decision-making through a framework of theories, techniques and models.

Strategy decisions

Ansoff identified four standard types of organisational decisions: strategy, policy, programmes and standard operating procedures. The last three, he argued, are designed to resolve recurring problems or issues and, once formulated, do not require an original decision each time. This means that the decision process can easily be delegated. Strategy decisions are different, however, because they always apply to new situations and so need to be made anew every time.

Ansoff developed a new classification of decision-making, partially based on Alfred Chandler's work in *Strategy and Structure* (1962). This distinguished decisions as strategic (focused on the areas of products and markets), administrative (organisational and resource allocating), or operating (budgeting and directly managing). Ansoff's decision classification became known as strategy-structure-systems, or the 3S model. (Sumantra Ghoshal later proposed a 3Ps model – purpose, process and people – to replace it.)

Components of strategy

Ansoff argued that within a company's activities there should be an element of core capability, an idea later adopted and expanded by Gary Hamel and C. K. Prahalad. To establish a link between past and future corporate activities (the first time such an approach was undertaken), Ansoff identified four key strategy components:

- **product-market scope** – a clear idea of what business or products a company was responsible for (pre-dating the exhortations of Tom Peters and Robert Waterman to 'stick to your knitting')

- **growth vector** – as explained in the section below on the Ansoff matrix, this offers a way of exploring how growth may be attempted

- **competitive advantage** – those advantages an organisation possesses that will enable it to compete effectively, a concept later championed by Michael Porter

- **synergy** – Ansoff explained synergy as $2 + 2 = 5$ (i.e. the whole is greater than the sum of the parts) and it requires an examination of how opportunities fit the core capabilities of the organisation.

Ansoff matrix

Variously known as the product-mission matrix or the 2 x 2 growth vector component matrix, the Ansoff matrix remains a popular tool for organisations that wish to understand the risk component of various growth strategies, including product versus market development, and diversification. The matrix was first published in a 1957 article, 'Strategies for diversification'; Figure 5 shows what such a matrix may look like.

Of the four strategies given in the matrix, market penetration requires increasing existing product market share in existing markets; market expansion requires the identification of new customers for existing products; product expansion

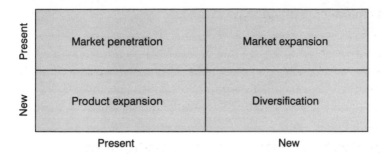

Figure 5: The Ansoff matrix

requires developing new products for existing customers; and diversification requires new products to be produced for new markets.

Ansoff's article focused particularly on diversification as a potentially high-growth but also high-risk strategy requiring careful planning and analysis before any decision is taken. He viewed diversification as a particularly important growth strategy, requiring organisations to 'break with past patterns and traditions' as they go along new 'uncharted paths' where, generally, new skills, techniques and resources will be required. His matrix offered a method of carefully analysing and evaluating the profit potential of diversification strategies.

Paralysis by analysis

It has sometimes been suggested that the application of the ideas in *Corporate Strategy* can lead to too much emphasis on analysis. Ansoff himself recognised this possibility, however, and coined the now famous phrase 'paralysis by analysis' to describe the type of procrastination caused by excessive planning.

Turbulence

The issue of turbulence underlies all Ansoff's work on strategy. One of his aims in establishing a better framework for strategy formulation was to improve the existing planning processes of the stable, post-war economy of the US, since he realised these would not be sufficient to cope with pressures that rapid and discontinuous change would place on them.

By the 1980s change, and the pace of change, had become a key issue for management in most organisations. Ansoff recognised, however, that while some organisations were faced with conditions of great turbulence, others still operated in relatively stable conditions. Consequently, although strategy formulation had to take environmental turbulence into account, one strategy could not be made to fit every industry. These ideas are discussed in *Implanting Strategic Management*, where five levels of environmental turbulence are outlined:

- **repetitive** – change is slow and predictable
- **expanding** – the marketplace is stable, growing gradually
- **changing** – incremental growth, with customer requirements altering fairly quickly
- **discontinuous** – some predictable change and some more complex change
- **surprising** – change that cannot be predicted that both develops, and develops from, new products or services.

In perspective

Although other strategists frequently refer to Ansoff's work, it has not become more generally recognised in comparison with that of other theorists. The complexity of his work and its reliance on the disciplines of analysis and planning are perhaps among the reasons Ansoff is not popularly viewed as being in the top echelon of management thinkers.

Other theorists were working on similar themes at similar times to Ansoff. In the 1960s, his notion of competence (which was later developed by Hamel and Prahalad) was not unique, and although Ansoff seems to have been the originator of the 2 x 2 growth vector component matrix, a similar matrix had been published earlier. During the 1980s and 1990s, it is likely that much work by other theorists about strategy formation under conditions of uncertainty or chaos owed something to Ansoff's theory of turbulence, though it is difficult to evaluate the extent of the debt.

A debate between Ansoff and Henry Mintzberg over their differing views of strategy was reflected in print over many years, particularly in *Harvard Business Review*. Ansoff has often been criticised by Mintzberg, who disliked the idea of strategy being built from planning that is supported by analytical techniques. This criticism was based on the belief that Ansoff's reliance on planning suffered from three fallacies: that events can be predicted; that strategic thinking can be separated from operational management; and that hard data, analysis and techniques can produce novel strategies.

Ansoff was one of the earliest writers on strategy as a management discipline, and laid strong foundations for several later writers to build upon, including Porter, Hamel and Prahalad. He invented the modern approach to strategy and his work pulled together various ideas and disparate strands of thought, giving a new coherence and discipline to the concept he described as strategic planning. During the 1970s and 1980s, this concept shaped more theories about management as other writers took up Ansoff's ideas, such as core competence or 'sticking to your knitting'.

Developing strategy

There are many definitions of strategy. Perhaps the simplest is the direction an organisation takes with the aim of achieving future business success.

Strategy sets out how an organisation intends to employ its resources, including the skills and knowledge of its people as well as financial and material assets, to achieve its mission or overall objectives and its vision.

There is a fine line between mission and vision and the terms are not always used in the same way. Generally, however, mission focuses primarily on an organisation's purpose, the reason it exists, and corporate vision is an image of the future to which an organisation aspires.

Strategy development is the process of researching and identifying strategic options, selecting the most promising and deciding how resources will be allocated across the organisation to achieve objectives. Some of the key questions an organisation needs to ask in connection with its future are as follows:

- What business are we in? Or what business should we be in? (Mission)
- Where do we want to be? (Vision)
- How are we doing? What is going well? What is not so successful?
- How did we get to this point? What went well? What went wrong?
- How can we improve our position?

- What options are open to us?
- What might hinder us from getting there?
- What do we need to do to get there?
- What should we not do?

It has been said that in strategy everything is simple but nothing is easy. At times of economic turbulence, environmental uncertainty and growing complexity, how organisations can best set their direction for the future remains an enduring subject of debate and interest.

In the past, most organisations took a highly structured approach to strategy development known as strategic planning. This was an annual process of putting plans in place for the coming year and beyond. However, in today's complex and turbulent business environment, it is impossible to plan for every eventuality and strategy-making needs to be a more flexible and dynamic process, reflecting a way of thinking strategically about the business and the environment in which it operates. Organisations that fail to think strategically are vulnerable to threats and ill-prepared to take advantage of fresh opportunities. A flexible but focused approach puts organisations in a better position to deal with setbacks and to respond to new opportunities as they emerge. Nonetheless, organisations still need to gain a clear understanding of the marketplace and their strategic position within it. Analysis and planning remain important for the majority of them.

There are many models of and approaches to strategy and a plethora of tools and techniques to help strategy-makers assess their current position and evaluate options for the future. Such tools should not be regarded as recipes for success; they should be used with careful thought to help analyse and understand an organisation's strategic context.

Failing to think strategically means that an organisation will become reactive, vulnerable to threats and closed to opportunities. Organisational strategy needs to be:

- **flexible** – adaptable to change, but in line with corporate mission and vision
- **responsive** – taking account of market, economic and environmental conditions
- **creative** – to inspire commitment and ensure the organisation stands out from the crowd
- **challenging** – so that it acts as a source of inspiration and motivation
- **realistic** – so that it can be seen to be achievable and people can get to grips with it
- **focused** – clear, defined and understandable to all stakeholders, especially employees and customers
- **engaging** – in line with organisational culture and values.

This checklist provides a framework for thinking about and developing organisational strategy. It is based broadly on established processes of analysis, choice and implementation.

Strategy development is often seen as predominantly the responsibility of senior management. However, in some cases, senior managers set the strategic direction and divisional heads will then be given responsibility for developing appropriate strategies for their parts of the business. Moreover, all managers have a role to play in implementing and shaping strategy and in gaining acceptance from the teams that will be executing the strategy day to day. It is important for managers to develop their strategic awareness, to be aware of their organisation's current position and open to potential opportunities for change and development.

Action checklist

1 Understand the current position

Start with an assessment of the organisation's current position. This involves looking at recent performance and position in the marketplace.

Questions to ask include:

- What is our vision and how well-placed are we to deliver it?
- How is the organisation performing?
- What is going well and what is not going so well?
- What is our market share?
- How are we placed in relation to our competitors?
- How do our customers see us?
- Are we on an upward or a downward curve?

Try to form a balanced view of the organisation, not just the rosy side. Do not make assumptions – seek evidence so that decisions and future plans are based on reality.

2 Reflect on how you got there

Based on analysis of the current position, consider the reasons behind successes and failures. Are these a result of market forces, for example, or are they the result of internal strengths or weaknesses? Questions to ask include:

- What did we do right (wrong) to get there?
- What have we done well (or badly)?
- Were we in the right place at the right time?
- What was a consequence of market circumstances?
- What was a result of good planning, bad planning, or lack of planning?

3 Be clear about your corporate identity (mission, vision and values)

Revisit any existing statements of the organisation's mission – its purpose and what it exists for, its vision – what it aspires to achieve and its values – the manner in which it believes it should do business. Are these still appropriate and valid? Consider whether your perspective needs to broaden to take advantage of fresh opportunities or be narrowed to maintain focus and effectiveness.

Try to gain a clear sense of identity by asking questions such as:

- What kind of organisation are we?
- What does our vision indicate that we need to focus on?
- What kind of values do we have? Are we living them out or have we lost track of them?
- What people strengths (or weaknesses) do we have?
- What kind of leadership do we have?
- What is the level of morale?

4 Analyse your strengths and weaknesses

SWOT analysis, which focuses on assessing organisational strengths and weaknesses as well as threats and opportunities, is a popular tool which can help to focus attention on an organisation's capabilities and identify factors that could limit its achievements.

A review of the strengths and weaknesses of the current portfolio of products and/or services offered by the organisation should also be included. The Boston matrix provides a framework for assessing the current and potential performance of products or services and can help to guide decisions on which are worth investing in for the future.

5 Analyse the business environment

The PEST analysis tool, which is used by many organisations to help them get an overview of the current and future business environment in which they are operating, traditionally focused on political, economic, social and technological factors. A number of variants such as PESTLE and PEST-C have evolved to include additional factors such as legal, environmental and cultural.

Questions to ask include:

- What are the major trends likely to affect our business?

- What new technologies are available?
- How are customer needs and attitudes changing and evolving?

  Pay particular attention to identifying the driving forces in your sector. These are the major underlying causes of changing competitive conditions. The most common are:

- changes in long-term industry growth rates
- increasing globalisation
- product innovation
- the strength and number of existing and emerging competitors
- the entry or exit of major firms in the sector.

  Porter's five forces model can help to assess the factors affecting the competitive position of an organisation.

6 Identify and evaluate strategic options

A clear understanding of the current position should generate insights that will help an organisation identify the most promising strategic choices. Factors to be considered include:

- how performance can be improved
- what changes or adjustments in direction are needed
- whether the situation calls for a widening or narrowing of focus
- whether it is feasible to expand into new markets
- which market areas offer the best chances of success
- whether existing products and services can be improved or updated
- when new products and services need to be introduced
- what scope there is for innovation in processes
- how the competition can best be tackled
- what organisational development initiatives may be needed
- whether there are things the organisation needs to stop doing.

When evaluating strategic options, consider the conditions that must be true for the strategy to be successful and identify barriers to success. In some cases it may be possible to conduct tests to gauge the likelihood of specific scenarios, but bear in mind that the future is never certain. In recent years there has been a growing emphasis on the benefits of combining the results of rational analysis with the experience and intuition of strategic leaders.

It is important for organisational strategies to take account of identified weaknesses and to provide a framework for addressing them, as well as capitalising on organisational strengths. For each option, consider the investment and resources that will be required and their availability. This should include:

- people skills which will need to be developed or brought in
- equipment and technology infrastructure
- production and distribution capacity.

Time frames should also be discussed. These vary hugely from sector to sector. For example, internet businesses are evolving fast, but companies in the energy sector, where exploration and infrastructure development are involved, need to take a much longer-term view. Although it takes time to change thinking and shift resources, in general tighter time frames are being set for targets than in the past.

7 Set objectives

Once the strategic direction has been agreed, it is crucial to translate this into specific objectives. These need to be firm without being so rigid that any modifications will result in failure. Objectives should be set by considering how the strategy is to be realised and what, in measurable terms, needs to happen if it is to be successful.

The following aspects should be covered:

- profitability and return on investment

- market share and market needs
- product/service quality and customer service
- changes needed to organisational processes, activities and culture
- social responsibility
- people participation and commitment.

8 Communicate the strategy

Communicate details of the thinking that is emerging throughout the organisation. This will involve clearly documenting strategic decisions and adjustments as they are made. All employees, and especially managers, need to be fully aware of organisational strategy and to understand how their own job roles contribute to the achievement of organisational objectives. Widespread consultation and feedback will help to gain commitment, but will also facilitate the gathering of additional information on threats and opportunities from those who work on the front line.

9 Implement the strategy

In recent years there has been a growing awareness that it is one thing to formulate a strategy but another to implement it. Unless the practical implications are worked out and acted on, the strategy will be no more than a statement of hopes and aspirations for the future. A clear route map needs to be outlined with time frames and staging posts. If objectives are to be achieved, everyone in the organisation should have a clear understanding of what needs to be done, when and by whom. Depending on the size of the organisation, the implications of the strategy for business and operational plans, marketing plans, financial plans and budgets, project plans and personal development plans need to be clarified and the steps that need to be taken identified.

10 Review progress

The end point of strategic action is a combination of products and services, employees, customers and technologies that produce results. The one constant is the need to stay close to the market. This involves continuing measurement of progress against objectives; continuing assessment of the market and business environment or the needs and requirements of stakeholders; and continuing adjustment to changing circumstances to take advantage of changing technologies and explore new opportunities as they become apparent.

As a manager you should avoid:

- forgetting to spend time getting to know your industry/market sector

- being unaware of core strengths and critical factors

- assuming that you know what your customers need and want.

Setting objectives

An objective is an end towards which effort is directed and resources are focused. Terminology varies and there is sometimes confusion over the use of terms such as objectives, aims, policy, goals and targets. It is important that everyone in an organisation understands the meaning of the terms used. The term 'objective' is used throughout this checklist.

This checklist is intended for managers who participate in setting corporate objectives, or who interpret and apply such objectives to their own functional or departmental areas of responsibility.

Setting corporate objectives involves clarifying the strategic aims and policy requirements of the organisation and agreeing related complementary operational objectives. This is an integrated process that links corporate planning or strategy-making to business operations and organisation structure. Objectives may be long-term and high-level or short-term and low-level. As objectives are cascaded through the organisation they usually become more specific, with clearly defined areas of application and time limits. Every department, unit, team and individual should have clear and meaningful objectives.

For objectives to be achieved successfully it is necessary to identify clear areas of responsibility, such as improving performance or service, and to prioritise objectives as essential or desirable. Write a statement of objectives that are SMART: specific, measurable, action-oriented, realistic, time- (and resource-) constrained. All objectives should be subject to a process of discussion and agreement with those members of staff responsible for their achievement. When staff members are involved in agreeing objectives, it is easier for them to take ownership of them and more likely to lead to commitment and successful achievement.

Be aware that if you fail to set objectives, you risk not knowing how or whether what you are doing fits in with your organisation's longer-term plans or higher-level objectives. This can result in confusion and lowered morale, and it will be difficult to assess how successful you have been in managing personal, team or organisational performance.

Action checklist

1 Develop and communicate the organisation's mission and vision

People often confuse mission and vision statements. It is possible, and even desirable, to have objectives relating to both.

The mission statement expresses the reason an organisation exists (e.g. to make top-quality cars) and provides an umbrella statement of its standing objectives. Typically this mission is enduring and changes little (unless the organisation undergoes radical re-engineering or a change of context).

The vision statement is an expression of the end result to which the organisation aspires. Typically, it provides guidance on timescale and measurable outcomes or indicators. For example: 'Our aim is to become the largest-selling car manufacturer in the world by 2020.' Such statements should be clearly communicated and reinforced with all employees, not just senior managers.

2 Identify corporate objectives from the mission/vision statements

It is important to link corporate objectives with mission and vision statements. This helps individuals see the importance, relevance and value of objectives and thus reinforces commitment to achieving them.

Formulating organisational strategy and objectives is normally the responsibility of senior management, but in empowered organisations this process may be delegated to other staff members. Some organisations use a bottom-up process to gauge achievability at the delivery level. This has the advantage of promoting personal commitment to objectives with an element of team contribution and monitoring.

The strategy is formulated by an assessment of:

- what the organisation intends to accomplish and where it aims to be in the future
- how it can position itself in the right place at the right time with the right product(s) and/or service(s)
- how it can be successful and sustainable in the long term.

Much will depend on the organisation's values, as these express what is important to it – for example, its employees, its public image, or its environment. Objectives and strategies for achieving them should be governed by the organisation's values. Be aware that setting new high-level objectives could challenge organisational values (or change them).

It is important to make sure that the set of objectives for any function, team or individual is truly representative of the things that matter most to the organisation. The objectives that are agreed will draw attention and effort, and you do not want effort to be misdirected or important aspects of work performance to be neglected because they have not been included in the objectives.

3 Agree objectives for senior managers

This involves allocating the corporate objectives by function, business unit and/or by product or service. You should prioritise the objectives, create time frames and confirm the resources required to meet them.

4 Agree objectives with those who are to tackle them

Objective setting should not be undertaken by order or command. The ideal process is one of proposing and seeking ideas, discussion, negotiation and agreement. Remember Kipling's six honest serving men: who, what, where, when, why and how. Answering these questions is the minimum that both manager and job holder should require from a one-to-one meeting. Equally, this should not be a process by which objectives are overly diluted – the purpose is to stretch performance towards a desirable future.

5 Identify appropriate performance measures

Wherever possible, quantitative performance measures should enable progress to be monitored against objectives to create a baseline of achievement. If such measures are not possible, another means of monitoring progress should be established.

Performance measures (which can be employed on a team or individual basis) should indicate what is expected and how well people are doing in meeting their objectives. Such measures should be clear, concise, easy to collect and interpret, and relevant, in that they should provide information that shows you and your organisation how well you are performing.

Performance measures should relate to:

- efficiency – attention given to the right objectives
- effectiveness – attention to what is actually accomplished within a given time period.

Performance measures usually cover information related to:

- finance – budget headings, costs and income
- customers – past, present and new
- market penetration
- resources – consumed, saved or required.

It is generally agreed that, to achieve optimum levels of

motivation, it is desirable for managers and staff to be able both to track their progress towards key milestones and to discern the impact of actions taken to deliver objectives and vision. Many organisations use key performance indicators (KPIs) to track this in a range of significant, relevant and representative ways; others use scorecards such as the balanced scorecard developed by Robert Kaplan and David Norton.

6 Set up procedures for reviewing performance

Managers may need time to help staff understand and interpret their objectives and the contribution they make to corporate strategy. Objectives and the related performance measures should be subject to review, especially if there are significant changes at the environmental or organisational level, or in the nature of the work to be carried out. An honest appraisal of past performance provides learning opportunities and a basis for agreement on revised or new objectives. Regular reviews of progress are beneficial both for the organisation and for individual personal development.

As a manager you should avoid:

- excluding those who are responsible for achieving objectives from the process of discussing and agreeing them
- failing to restart the cycle by reviewing and revising objectives
- being unclear as to the direction the organisation is going in.

Implementing strategy

Strategy implementation is the process by which an organisation translates its chosen strategy into action plans and activities, which will steer it in the direction set out in the strategy and enable it to achieve its strategic objectives.

The development of organisational strategy is a complex and demanding process, and leaders who have devoted time, effort and resources to the selection of a strategy that they believe will secure the success of their company may feel they have good reason to be confident about the future. Nonetheless, their chosen strategy stands little chance of success unless it is acted on. Effective implementation is critical to the success of organisational strategy.

If strategy is to be more than an expression of hopes and aspirations for the future, the practical implications for organisational operations and activities must be thought through and put into practice. Strategy implementation requires organisations to put initiatives in place that are focused and realisable. A strategic focus should encourage them to develop disciplined processes for feeding strategic initiatives across the organisation in a meaningful, realistic and achievable way.

The implementation or execution of strategy, however, is often neglected and its results are frequently unpredictable. Problems encountered in the implementation of strategy often lie not in any flaws in the strategy itself, but rather in a failure to implement it effectively. Such failures can mean that strategic initiatives are only partially successful and lead to frustration, as the hoped-for strategic benefits are not realised. Ultimately, they can result in the decline or even failure of the business as a whole.

Translating strategy aims into actionable processes in an ordered fashion, however, is not easy. The setting of priorities and the development of plans may present organisations with formidable management challenges. The effective execution of strategy can be impeded by many and varied difficulties, such as weak or inconsistent senior-level commitment, a lack of support from managers and employees, cross-departmental conflicts, ambiguity in roles and responsibilities, or a lack of accountability.

This checklist aims to help managers understand the complexities of strategy implementation and provide guidance on the factors that will help organisations achieve optimal, rather than maximal, implementation of strategy.

Action checklist

1 Ensure that plans are aligned with organisational mission, vision and values

Strategic development is an important business activity that involves defining the strategic direction an organisation will take and the objectives it aims to achieve. Obvious as this may seem, it is important to ensure that implementation plans are based on the stated organisational strategy and objectives. Just as strategy must be derived from the organisation's mission and vision and in line with organisational values, so implementation must follow the direction set out in the organisation's strategic documents and prioritise those things which are seen to be most important for its future success. Bear in mind, however, that organisational mission and vision, or even values, may need to change in response to changing circumstances and should be reviewed regularly.

2 Build an effective leadership team

The optimal implementation of strategy depends on the people-management and leadership capabilities of both strategic and operational managers. New strategies may create new requirements for leaders and the organisations they lead. Strategic change may require new personnel with fresh perspectives, or differing skills and experience. Strategic shifts may well entail a change in emphasis involving new customers or markets, technologies or business processes. Leaders may need to adjust their leadership styles, or learn new management techniques and approaches. The implementation of a new strategy may alter priorities, change resource allocations and involve a shift in relationships. This can sometimes pose a threat to the power and status of influential people within the organisation.

Processes for assessing and developing leadership should be seen as a normal part of strategic implementation. Leaders must take an objective view of the existing management team, including themselves, and assess whether it is capable of implementing the strategy. Ideally, coaching or development should be offered to help individuals improve their performance or develop new skills, if necessary, so that they are better able to achieve the required goals and objectives. Some people may be incapable of adapting, resistant to change, or unwilling to accept a revised role and prefer to move on to another organisation. These are sensitive issues that must be handled carefully, with due regard for legislation relating to issues such as redundancy and constructive dismissal.

Building the right team is crucial to the success of strategy execution. Organisations need to have HR personnel and processes in place to recruit new people as required. The selection of team members should not, however, lie solely with the HR department but must involve senior management. This will reinforce the importance of the initiative and can also be a means of identifying talent within an organisation. Involvement in implementation teams should be seen as a positive career move.

3 Create an implementation plan

A full implementation plan with milestones needs to be created for all levels of the organisation. The plan should outline the steps necessary to achieve the objectives and include schedules for key activities. The resources needed to achieve the objectives must also be detailed. The plan should quantify the financial, personnel, operational, time and technological resources required, and identify those responsible for individual initiatives.

The implementation plan sets priorities and accountabilities, including short-term and long-term objectives. Strategic objectives should be broken down into manageable pieces and establish a chain of command; they may also outline additional organisational structures that need to be aligned with the strategy initiative, such as cross-functional teams. Accountability is an important factor in successfully delivering strategy and acts as a motivator, concentrating people's minds on following through on the responsibilities allocated to them. Personal accountability must be clearly defined so that individuals understand what they are responsible for.

A fundamental task when drawing up a strategic implementation plan is to draft it in such a way that it can be split into separate action plans for each project and initiative. Make sure that good project management practices are followed and that training in project management methods is given where appropriate. The plan also needs to be visible, so that it does not become disconnected from the decision-making process, and accessible to all, not restricted to the strategy department or senior managers.

Strategy implementation is a dynamic process that has to take account of changing conditions affecting the strategy and its implementation. You must be able to change and amend the plan as circumstances dictate and the latest version should incorporate the results of ongoing learning.

4 Allocate budgetary resources

Securing a satisfactory budget is one of the main requirements when implementing strategy. A new strategy may entail the development of new processes, the purchase of new equipment, the recruitment of additional employees, staff training or development activities, or the upgrading of information technology. The budgeting process needs to ensure that strategic initiatives are properly resourced and can be implemented in the agreed timescales.

Organisations use budgets to make sure that what is important gets done, but it is all too easy to focus on tactical challenges and short-term financial targets and allow this to take up a large amount of time and resources. Strategic initiatives can become victims of this process, so the budgetary process must be aligned with strategy. Each aspect of the strategy must be linked to operating and capital budgets.

Budgetary processes can also be used to track whether activities are behind schedule or not achieving the anticipated results. Financial forecasts, key performance indicators (KPIs) and actual expenditure can be compared to assess progress and decide whether the costs involved are worth the results being produced. In some cases, it may become necessary to adjust the budget in order to reallocate or redistribute resources and get the strategy back on track.

5 Assign objectives and responsibilities

A formal planning and measurement structure is needed to implement strategy effectively. Strategic responsibilities and objectives must be clearly assigned so that individuals understand their roles within the strategy and are able to take responsibility for or ownership of specific strategic tasks and outcomes. All those who have a role to play in the implementation of the strategy need to be clear about intended outcomes and their responsibilities for the achievement of these. Making sure that employees know and understand their roles and how these contribute to organisational objectives is the job of those who have drawn up the strategy and those who are responsible for ensuring that it is being implemented effectively.

Objectives and responsibilities should be made explicit, and where possible they should be assigned to individuals rather than teams, as this makes for clear personal accountability. Employees at all levels also need to know how their performance will be measured and evaluated. Measures should be created for each task and documented, so that everybody knows what the intended outcomes and the expected time frames are. Organisations will be unable to hold individuals to account if strategic objectives or outcomes are not measured.

It is important to break strategic goals down into smaller objectives that can be measured and tracked. Meeting specific objectives step by step will give individuals and teams a sense of achievement, generate a sense of momentum and help to maintain enthusiasm. Be aware that some outcomes, such as a growth in profits, are relatively easy to record and measure, but others, such as staff morale and engagement, will require softer measures.

6 Align structures and processes

All organisations have existing business processes, plans and structures in place to manage their operations. Often these operate in isolation and bear little relation to each other or to organisational strategy. If separate business units set their objectives independently, the contribution they make to organisational success could well turn out to be less than expected.

For an organisation to be capable of effectively implementing strategy, structures and processes need to be aligned with the strategic objectives. The strategy may be set out in a plan, but organisational structures will determine how it is defined and executed. The activities of business units need to be coordinated and the skills and capabilities of each unit made available for the benefit of the organisation as a whole. Think about how this can be achieved – perhaps by individual directors championing a particular strand of the business across the organisation. Alignment assists in clarifying the strategy and in coordinating the activities of those who put it into action. It also ensures consistency of purpose from the top of the organisation down to the operating level as strategy is embedded throughout the organisation.

Ongoing and proposed projects also need to be aligned with strategic objectives. To achieve this, each project must be evaluated to determine whether and to what extent it will contribute to the achievement of strategic objectives. This will inform decisions as to which projects should be resourced and carried through to completion. Review points should be built into implementation plans.

7 Align people

Effective people management is a critical issue in the successful implementation of strategy. The work of employees needs to be aligned with the strategy, so that their efforts contribute to the achievement of organisational objectives. Organisations should define the behaviour required throughout the organisation. It may be necessary to ask employees to change the way they work, in which case cultural issues need to be considered. For example, in organisations where internal collaboration has traditionally been weak, employees may need to start working cross-functionally.

Organisations need to create a cohesive strategy that employees can understand and engage with. Employees need to know that they are making a meaningful contribution to the success of the organisation, and senior leaders must make sure that employees at all levels can articulate and evaluate how their personal job roles help to achieve specific strategic objectives.

Organisations should think about the skills and capabilities they need to meet their strategic aims, both now and in the future. For this reason, leaders should attempt to anticipate how the organisation and the strategy are likely to evolve in the foreseeable future and identify skills that will be of greater or lesser importance.

8 Communicate the strategy

All employees should have a clear understanding of the core elements of the strategy and how it is to be executed, so it must be effectively communicated. This will encourage employee buy-in, commitment and engagement and should have a positive impact on productivity. Develop a communication strategy that will promote the overall vision and strategy of the organisation and formulate a set of well-defined goals. Avoid vague statements and make sure that objectives are expressed in concrete and measurable terms with tangible results and expected time frames.

Issues to be considered include the messages to be communicated, audience to be reached, behavioural changes needed, communication channels to be used and measures to evaluate the level of success or failure. Simply giving employees a copy of the strategy plan is rarely effective. Instead, prepare a separate document, providing a clear, concise summary of the most important points. Remember to include information on why this particular strategy has been adopted and explain the rationale for the priorities that have been established. Avoid jargon and aim to make the message clear, concise, consistent, and as convincing and compelling as possible.

To ensure that the message becomes embedded, be prepared to repeat it often, possibly using different channels, media and formats. Aligning your communications with organisational objectives will make them more relevant and effective, and help you make a convincing case for the resourcing of communications activity within the organisation. In the case of a long-term strategy, identify some quick wins to demonstrate the success of the new strategy and increase the visibility of the changes at regular intervals.

9 Review and report on progress

Progress should be reviewed regularly to check that the strategy is being implemented as envisioned. Strategy reviews allow managers to track progress, reflect on priorities and identify any issues that may need to be tackled. Remember, though, that strategy reviews have more to do with whether the strategy is producing results than with controlling performance.

Review meetings must be held often enough to keep the implementation process on course and enable leaders to take decisions about any strategic adjustments that need to be made. Initially, this may be weekly, fortnightly, monthly or quarterly. Frequency can be scaled back later when it is clear that the implementation process has been established and is working well. More frequent meetings may be necessary if the strategy is introducing major organisational change or if the business environment is evolving rapidly. There must be sufficient time for meaningful discussion to take place. Meetings may be time-consuming at first but the need for frequent meetings will decrease. Time spent productively in the early stages will save time later on.

The regular reporting and reviewing process should be supported by an effective tracking system that describes and measures performance. Such measures, or KPIs, can be developed using a framework such as Kaplan and Norton's balanced scorecard. This uses financial and non-financial perspectives to describe progress in consistent, insightful operational terms and to translate strategic objectives into measurable performance. The use of such a framework can facilitate improvements as the effectiveness of the strategy is tested in the real world.

10 Make strategic adjustments as necessary

Strategy implementation is a dynamic process that takes place against a background of changing economic, social and competitive circumstances. This is where the leadership skills, capabilities and judgement of managers are needed to steer the organisation, underlining what was said in point 2 about the importance of building a good leadership team. This will involve decisions on the allocation of resources for optimal benefits as the competitive context evolves, and judgements as to when changes are warranted. A balance between frequent changes of direction, which may result in loss of organisational momentum and coordination, and rigid adherence to plans, when these are manifestly not achieving results, needs to be found. Just as important is the need for managers to align people, communicating changes, explaining how individual and team efforts contribute to outcomes and how engagement with the strategy will help them to achieve personal goals and aspirations, and effectively motivating and energising employees across the organisation.

11 Develop an organisational culture that supports the strategy

Organisational culture plays a significant role in translating strategic plans and initiatives into action. No matter how good an organisation's strategy may be, implementation will be hindered if the organisational culture does not support it.

Culture is to an organisation what personality and character are to individuals. It consists of the assumptions, values and beliefs that employees share and that influence their activities, opinions and behaviour at work. A culture that is aligned with organisational strategy will help organisations implement strategy successfully, as a shared belief in organisational aims and objectives will promote commitment. Conversely, an organisational culture that is not aligned may stand in the way of adjustments to changing business needs and weaken the ability of an organisation to achieve its strategic aims.

As a manager you should avoid:

- thinking that strategy implementation is a simple process

- being caught unawares by unanticipated market changes which necessitate adjustments
- committing insufficient resources to execute the strategy
- failing to align organisational design and capabilities with the strategy
- failing to communicate the strategy consistently and persistently throughout the organisation
- making the strategy implementation and reporting process overly bureaucratic and time-consuming, leaving little time to put real changes into action.

Gary Hamel

The search for a new strategic platform

Introduction

Gary Hamel (b. 1954) is one of the most respected contributors to the debate on strategy of the late 20th century. His fresh and often hard-hitting approach to organisational innovation and reinvention has brought wide acknowledgement from academics and practitioners alike.

Hamel's reputation developed from the early 1990s when, with C. K. Prahalad, he began to communicate his revolutionary views on strategy, in the process creating the concepts of organisational core competences, strategic intent and strategic architecture. In an article in *Sloan Management Review* (1998), 'Strategy innovation and the quest for value', he said:

Gastric upset is at least as likely to produce a strategy insight as attendance at another interminable planning meeting.

Life and career

Hamel worked as a hospital administrator until 1978, when he began to study for a PhD in international business at the University of Michigan. There he met Prahalad, who later became his mentor, collaborator and colleague in research, writing and business. Hamel first came to prominence through journal articles in the early 1990s and as the co-author of a book, *Competing for the Future* (1994), written (like most of the articles) with Prahalad.

Now at the forefront of thinking on strategy, Hamel is visiting professor in strategic and international management at London Business School, distinguished research fellow at Harvard Business School and chairman of Strategos, a strategy services company he set up with Prahalad in 1995. Hamel is also a fellow of the World Economic Forum and the Strategic Management Society.

Together with Julian Birkinshaw, Hamel led a project to build the Management Innovation Lab (MLab). In collaboration with leading organisations and management scholars, MLab aims to create 'tomorrow's best practices' today and make a significant contribution towards the evolution of management knowledge and practice.

Key theories

Why a new approach to strategy?

At the beginning of the 1980s, Hamel argues, organisational development was no longer driven by strategic forces but by incrementalism. Companies were concerned with getting bigger and better through downsizing, delayering, re-engineering and continuous quality improvements, and their goal became to mimic best practice. The result of these incremental improvements was to squeeze cost efficiencies to the point where there was nothing left to gain.

At the same time, there were various new forces at work that were changing the nature of competition and the base of traditional industries, which had enjoyed primacy in the past. These forces included:

- deregulation and privatisation, particularly in the airline, telecommunications and financial services sectors
- blurring, fragmentation and growth of newcomers in the computer and telecommunications industries
- changing customer expectations in terms of price, quality and service

- discontinuous technological growth, particularly with the internet
- shifting boundaries of control and authority, as workforces became more widely distributed, more empowered and less layered
- changes in traditional loyalties, as people became simultaneously the most valuable, but also the most expendable, asset
- the lowered value of experience, as change undermines its relevance for the future.

Strategic questions to address

Hamel argues that a compelling view of the future is necessary if businesses are not to be tied to the orthodoxies of the past, and highlights the number of companies that lost money because they stuck too long to the same game instead of trying to get ahead of it. While no view of the future can be accurate or perfect, a view of some sort is essential. This can be developed through addressing questions about how it would be possible to unleash the corporate imagination, turn technicians into dreamers, turn planners into strategists, and create an organisation that really lives and makes its decisions in the future.

In a 1996 article in *Strategic Management Journal*, 'Competing in the new economy: managing out of bounds' (written with Prahalad), Hamel agrees that while we can all recognise a great strategy once it has proven successful in action, we find it difficult to generate a great strategy in the first place. He argues that strategy generation is not a purely analytical process but is multifaceted, involving risk, gut feel, intuition and emotion, as well as analysis.

Strategy as core competence

The concept of corporate competencies was highlighted by Hamel and Prahalad in journal articles and in their book *Competing for the Future*. In the latter, they argued that, for too long, the organisational focus had been on the returns from individual business units as opposed to the conditions, processes and competencies that enabled those returns. Hamel and Prahalad define 'core competencies' as the collective learning in the organisation and, especially, the coordination of diverse production skills and integration of multiple streams of technologies. They ask organisations to look upon themselves as portfolios of core competencies by analysing what it is that they do better than others. Viewing the organisation as systems of activities and building blocks means asking:

- How does activity X significantly improve the end-product for the customer?
- Does activity X offer access to a range of applications and markets?
- What would happen to our competitiveness if we lost our strength in activity X?
- How difficult is it for others to imitate activity X and compete with us?

To realise the potential that core competencies create, an organisation's people must have the imagination to visualise new markets and the ability to move into them, ahead of the competition. One of the keys to core competencies and effective competition is, therefore, the process through which an organisation releases corporate imagination. One of the words that recurs increasingly throughout Hamel's writing is revolution.

Strategy as revolution

In a seminal *Harvard Business Review* article, 'Strategy as revolution' (1996), Hamel sets out ten principles which strategy generators should bear in mind:

- Strategic planning is not strategic. Rather, it is a calendar-driven ritual, involving plans and sub-plans, instead of something challenging and innovative that might lead to discovery.
- Strategy-making should be subversive. Great strategies come from challenging the status quo and doing something different. The late Anita Roddick, founder of the highly innovative Body

Shop, was quoted as saying: 'I watch where the cosmetics industry is going and then walk in the opposite direction.'

- The bottleneck is at the top of the bottle. The most powerful defenders of strategic orthodoxy are senior management, and strategy-making needs to be freed from the tyranny of their experience.

- Revolutionaries exist in every company. Let everyone have their voice, so that new and young as well as tried and tested contributors are part of strategy-making.

- Change is not the problem – engagement is. People will support change and will welcome the responsibility for engendering it, if this gives them some control over their own future.

- Strategy-making must be democratic. The capability for strategic thinking is not limited to senior people, and it is impossible to predict where a good, revolutionary idea may be lurking.

- Anyone can be a strategy activist. People who care about their organisation do not wait for permission to act.

- Perspective is worth 50 IQ points. Subversive strategy means gaining a new perspective on the world, and looking at potential markets through new eyes, a new lens.

- Top-down and bottom-up are not alternatives. If top-down can achieve unity of purpose among the few involved, bottom-up will bring diversity of perspective. Bring the two together.

- You can't see the end from the beginning. Surprises do not appeal to everyone, but delving into discontinuities and identifying potential competencies will bring about unpredictable outcomes. These will probably not fit the orthodox strategic mould – but strategy-making is about letting go.

So how do we begin to put these principles into a framework for creating strategy as a systemic capability?

Creating strategy

In 'Strategy innovation and the quest for value' (cited above), Hamel said:

Strategy innovation is the only way for newcomers to succeed in the face of enormous resource disadvantages, and the only way for incumbents to renew their lease on success.

While some strategies result from analysis and others from inspiration and vision, many strategies also evolve and emerge. To achieve strategies that are neither too random nor too ordered or ritualistic, Hamel suggests we should look to the roots of strategy creation, which he regards as a relatively simple phenomenon amid the complexity of organisational life. In 'Strategy, innovation and the quest for value', Hamel turns his revolutionary principles into action points and urges organisations to adopt a new stance through the following:

- **New voices** – top management relinquishing its hold on strategy, and introducing newcomers; young people and people from different groups bringing richness and diversity to strategy formulation.

- **New conversations** – the same people talking about the same issues over and over again leads to sterility; new opportunities arise from juxtaposing formerly isolated people.

- **New passions** – people will go for change when they can steer it and benefit from it.

- **New perspectives** – search for new ways of looking at markets, customers and organisational capabilities; think different, see different.

- **New experiments** – small, low-risk experiments can accelerate the organisation's learning and will indicate what may work and what may not.

An agenda for management innovation

Leading the Revolution (2000) is a book about innovation. In it Hamel explores where revolutionary new business concepts come from and identifies the key design criteria for building activist-friendly and revolution-ready organisations. It is about throwing away the old rulebook, imagining a future that others have not seen, and then taking the initiative to act on it.

A later book, *The Future of Management* (co-authored with Bill Breen, 2007), also deals with innovation, setting out a bold agenda for 21st-century management transformation. Hamel suggests that modern management may have reached the 'limits of its improvability', being originally developed as a social technology to 'solve the problem of inefficiency'. Now, faced with an environment of constant change, organisations need to become 'as strategically adaptable as they are operationally efficient'. Hamel identifies three 'do or die' challenges facing organisations today and in the future:

- Dramatically accelerating the pace of strategic renewal in organisations large and small.
- Making innovation everyone's job, every day.
- Creating a highly engaging work environment that inspires employees to give the very best of themselves.

Hamel believes that the most successful organisations in the years to come will be the ones that have taken the lead in tackling these capstone challenges.

He goes on to identify new 21st-century management principles that he believes will be the key to the future of management. He considers these to be more effective than 20th-century principles of modern management in creating organisations that are adaptable and engaging. Hamel identifies the new principles by analysing aspects within an organisation that are already adaptable, innovative and highly engaging. Taking adaptability, for example, he draws inspiration from life, markets, democracies, religious faith and the world's most vibrant cities, all of which he sees as more resilient than large organisations.

Inspiration from	New principles
Life	Variety
Markets	Flexibility
Democracy	Activism
Faith	Meaning
Cities	Serendipity

In perspective

While it is not possible to pigeonhole Hamel, we can place him roughly in the progressive (if sometimes ragged) line of strategic thinking stretching back to Chandler and Ansoff, and including Porter and Mintzberg, as well as Hamel's collaborator and colleague Prahalad. Hamel continues to enjoy challenging convention and remains one of the most important contemporary business thinkers.

The role of the board in strategy

The board has a legal and commercial duty to promote the long-term health and stewardship of the company to the benefit of all stakeholders. Its role is a strategic one, ensuring full discussion and sound decisions on the major issues facing a company, such as regions and markets, technologies, appetite for risk, acceptable debt levels, and so on.

It is increasingly recognised that the role of the board in strategic management is of fundamental importance. There is an emerging consensus about its proper role within many businesses in the pages of *Harvard Business Review*, in the textbooks of leading governance advisers such as Ram Charan and Bob Garratt, and in the view of many successful board directors.

Nonetheless, there is research and anecdotal evidence that the strategic board is far from being a universal practice. Much of the difficulty lies in achieving a balance, making sure that the board is engaged and informed about the company's operations, but keeps to its strategic brief and does not dive into the day-to-day minutiae. The amount of legislation that companies have to comply with – not just corporate governance guidance, but the Sarbanes-Oxley law on financial compliance – means that it is easy for board meetings to become long exchanges of detailed information, rather than strategic discussions about market changes, product development, identifying necessary resources, emerging risks and scenario planning.

The role of the board has become particularly high-profile

following spectacular failures of strategic risk management in the past few decades, especially in financial services, and earlier in accountancy. There has been much criticism that reaction to scandals has focused too much on regulation and not enough on developing genuine strategic capability. Some aspects of corporate governance codes prescribe structural factors such as the proportion of 'independent' directors (those without executive responsibility), separation of the roles of chief executive and chairman, and so on. Many critics point out that compliance with these arrangements has little or no bearing on performance. The board's overriding priority should be the strategic direction of the company, good judgement and sound risk management.

The few research studies that have sought to identify the characteristics of effective boards strongly indicate that such boards are strongly engaged with the company but keep their intervention at the strategic level. It is possible now to talk in terms of a consensus on the characteristics of the strategic board, which this checklist sets out to summarise.

This is a simplification, but attitudes towards the role of the board have evolved over the decades. In the mid- to late 20th century, the idea of the powerful chief executive became popular, with the board's role seen as being somewhat arm's-length, even passive. Since the 1970s, growing concerns about the effectiveness of corporate governance have led to pressure on directors to play a more active role. Many commentators, however, say that this has resulted in engagement that is overzealous (too much intervention in day-to-day operational matters, too much discussion of the financial accounts), or too narrow (concentrating only on stock price, viewing the board's role as solely one of policing the executives). A consensus has evolved that the board should be engaged, but at a strategic level, considering the health and success of the company in the round.

Action checklist

1 Keep discussion strategic

This can be easy to conceptualise but hard to maintain. A strategic discussion concerns, for example, the opportunities and risks of expanding into new markets, rather than the logistics of a supply chain down to the smallest details. This can be hard to maintain, however, because sometimes board directors will need some level of detail if they have genuine concerns about an operation and want to be reassured on key aspects.

It helps to keep discussions at a strategic level if presentations by the executive team are succinct and focus on the big picture. CEOs can invite too much discussion of day-to-day detail by giving presentations consisting of numerous slides, heavy with financial and operational information.

2 Create a workable information architecture

Papers for board members should provide a clear summary, giving a strategic overview, but also include relevant detail and indicate where more information can be sourced.

Information should be qualitative as well as quantitative, including current information and future prospects as well as historic data. There should be information on employee engagement (and where possible more detailed analytics linking people-related investments to performance), on the customer experience, on competitors, and on technological and market developments. These reports should be as prominent and detailed as the traditional financial reports.

Executives should commit to keeping the board informed with regard to the implementation of strategy and the achievement of performance objectives.

3 Promote the concept of a 'learning board'

Companies continue to thrive if their rate of learning equals or exceeds the rate of change in their markets. Although a board role is part-time, it is nonetheless a professional task in its own right. Non-executive directors should commit to learning about the sector, its technology and market dynamics; and executive directors should see their board role as stewardship of the whole company, not as a means of representing their department's interests.

4 Encourage board members to commit to the company, not an interest group

The commercial and legal duty of the board is to the future health of the company. This is enshrined under company law in most jurisdictions, and reiterated in the UK in the Companies Act 2006. The board is not a representative of the shareholders or any particular interest group, although it does have a duty to promote the company's commercial success.

5 Directors have considerable responsibilities and equal status

Company law does not distinguish between 'independent' or non-executive directors and others – all have equal status. Garratt recommends that executive directors have two employment contracts: one for their executive responsibilities and one for their board responsibilities. All board members are equally responsible for the long-term stewardship of the company. They have considerable and specific legal responsibilities as board directors. It is advisable, therefore, that managers within the company who are not on the board do not have the term 'director' in their title, to avoid ambiguity.

Board members should commit to the company and set aside time commensurate to their responsibilities, not just show up for the meetings.

6 Facilitate and encourage communication between meetings

While board members should refrain from 'peering over the shoulders' of executives on a day-to-day basis, the most effective boards have communication between the executive team and other members between meetings. One means of facilitating this is a monthly letter – but again, it must stick to strategic matters.

7 Create space for deep strategic discussion

Meaningful strategy development involves an in-depth and informed discussion, which may be structured around the traditional SWOT (strengths, weaknesses, opportunities, threats) analysis. A common mistake, especially when there are many external or non-executive directors, is to focus too much on the externals (opportunities and threats) and not enough on internal matters. There need to be sufficient skills and resources to support bold strategic initiatives.

8 Discuss alternatives

Strategic discussion also involves choice. If a major strategic departure is considered, the merits not only of this but also of other courses of action should be discussed in depth. The danger of failing to do so is to fall victim to the latest business fad: 'Everyone's doing it; we should join in.'

9 Be prepared to challenge the 'difficult' board member

One of the most difficult matters to address in boardroom dynamics is the wasteful and time-consuming distraction of members who see board meetings as an opportunity to demonstrate their knowledge or create gratuitous conflicts. A strong chair should be capable of keeping the discussion to the principal strategic agenda and instilling a shared commitment to the company's well-being. Other discussions and debates can take place over lunch or evening drinks.

10 Create multiple objectives for CEO performance targets and pay

It is widely accepted that tying the chief executive's pay solely to movements in the stock price has created too much of a short-term focus, and probably also contributed to damaging and unethical practices such as mis-selling and, in financial services, excessive speculation. Multiple performance objectives, including some relating to qualitative matters such as the integrity of the company and the brand, help to encourage all-round leadership, and also to ensure that the board honours its overriding duty towards the company.

As a board member you should avoid:

- too much detail in presentations
- long papers without a clear summary
- lobbying for a particular department or other interest
- seeking to dominate the discussion, pursuing an issue that does not affect strategy
- promoting ambitious plans while neglecting the development of internal resources.

Brainstorming

Brainstorming is a technique for generating ideas, developing creativity, or solving problems in small groups through the free-flowing contributions of participants. Several variations of brainstorming and related techniques have emerged, such as brainwriting (where individuals write down their ideas), nominal group technique, electronic brainstorming and buzz discussion groups.

The purpose of this checklist is to enable a manager without previous experience of the technique and with a minimum of preparation to introduce brainstorming to a group and then go on to brainstorm a specific problem or opportunity.

Brainstorming can generate numerous fresh ideas and novel approaches, and can be fun and easy to learn. Despite controversy about the effectiveness of brainstorming groups compared with individual efforts at problem solving, brainstorming has many supporters. The use of a well-trained facilitator can overcome most difficulties or limitations and achieve additional benefits, such as enhanced member involvement and group interaction.

It is worth noting that to avoid offending people with conditions such as epilepsy, other terms such as 'thought showers' or 'cloud bursting' may be adopted, but the term 'brainstorming' is still widely used.

Action checklist: preparation

1 Select the problem or opportunity to be brainstormed

Select a topic important enough to justify the participation of others. This is likely to be something of particular importance to your organisation, perhaps a new product or strategic initiative. It should also be one with a number of possible solutions and where imagination and creative lateral thinking are required to identify these and assess their relative value.

2 Think about structure, aims and objectives

Although a brainstorming session has usually been thought of as an open, no-holds-barred event, establishing where you are going, what you want to achieve and broadly how you hope to get there is likely to provide a helpful framework. Some brainstorming sessions give participants some constraints to help them focus their minds, work more effectively and discover workable solutions. Whether or not you provide guidance and/ or restrictions, it is important to consider how to phrase the original question or topic. A clear and thought-provoking question can make a real difference to the quality of responses from the brainstorming group.

3 Choose a facilitator

Choosing the right facilitator is crucial. This should be an open, outgoing person with enthusiasm and the ability to stimulate interest and enjoyment. They need not be the most senior person at the session, but they will need to set the scene by creating an open atmosphere, controlling dominant people while encouraging participation from the more introverted group members, getting and keeping participants on track by highlighting the issues, and creating a sense of fun. Perhaps most importantly, they should be adept at keeping ideas flowing and be able to 'go with the flow' themselves.

Should the facilitator be internal or external? An external facilitator can be especially useful when senior managers are involved or confidentiality is required, but if the issue is not too complex or contentious, an internal facilitator may be used, provided they have some experience.

The facilitator should feel comfortable running activity-based sessions, and should have clear plans and tactics for arriving at particular outcomes or targets. The facilitator must also ensure, as much as possible, that the group members work as a team and take ownership of the ideas they come up with.

4 Select an appropriate venue

This depends largely on the time set aside for the session and the budget available. Somewhere away from the routine place of work is often more suitable and can help bring a fresh perspective to the discussion. Depending on the length of the session you may wish to provide refreshments at the venue – these can also act as an incentive to attend.

5 Consider the mix of participants

As well as people with a specialist contribution to make, include some who have little or no knowledge of the topic to be brainstormed. They will not be as familiar with the detail and will offer a fresh approach. Consider introducing outsiders, although this can backfire if they are seen as intruders or spies. A mix of representatives from different cultural backgrounds could be valuable to provide a range of perspectives on the issues to be discussed. Work on getting the group dynamics right in order to put the group at ease, avoid snide comments or put-downs, and create a blame-free atmosphere. All participants should be seen as equals and treated as such.

6 Decide on the number of participants

There is no right number, although more than ten might be unmanageable when ideas really start to flow and less than four might not be enough to generate creativity. Having a large group can inhibit participation by quieter members of the group and allow unwilling and unenthusiastic participants to avoid making a contribution. Four to eight is usually about right, although this will depend on the style of the facilitator and the nature of the issue to be tackled.

7 Get the equipment right

You will need some method of recording the ideas that come up. Audio and video recording may seem to be ideal for this, but participants can find these devices off-putting and recording can inhibit the free flow of ideas. A traditional flipchart and a plentiful supply of felt-tip pens are often adequate, with completed sheets tacked to the wall in full view to help stimulate further ideas. Consider also using technology such as laptops and projectors or interactive whiteboards, but make sure that all participants are clear on how to use the technology before the brainstorming session begins.

8 Get the layout right

Do not use a room with fixed rows of seats. Something more relaxed, even random, is preferable – a circle or U-shape is fairly common. The facilitator should check the room beforehand and prepare it appropriately.

9 Get the timing right

Reflect on your own powers of concentration and remember that in brainstorming sessions people can move from being dynamically engaged to feeling exhausted and back again. At least 10–20 minutes may be needed to get people relaxed. Two hours can be a long time to brainstorm – stop for a while if people show signs of tiredness. Arrange for a twenty-minute break after an hour's uninterrupted flow, or if and when the flow slows to a trickle. The break may be enough to stimulate an active restart, perhaps with a change in the seating of individuals.

10 Get the time of day right

It is difficult to give hard and fast advice on timing, as people differ. Some will function better after their routine work has been completed, when their minds are less preoccupied and they feel they can be more relaxed; others may prefer the morning when collective mental energy is at its highest.

11 Consider the role of pre-session brainstorming

Although brainstorming is often perceived as a spontaneous activity, you should provide sufficient notice of the session and, if possible, an outline of the problem to be tackled. This approach is likely to help people who like to have time to think through an idea and find it difficult to think on their feet.

You may also wish to ask participants to submit some initial ideas before the session begins. This can be done easily and anonymously using cloud computing technologies such as Google Drive. As well as being a preferred method of communication for introverts, doing this may help get the ball rolling at the official brainstorming session.

Action checklist: the session

1 State the topic or opportunity to be explored

State the topic and explain it to the group. Make sure everyone participating has a clear understanding of the issue and the objectives of the session. Ask participants if they have any initial questions and encourage them to behave in a courteous and constructive manner towards one another.

2 Restate the situation

Encourage the group to stand back from the topic, walk around it and see it from every angle. Suggest rewording it in 'how to' statements. Some restatements may be close to the original; others may illuminate new facets. Display these new statements on flipcharts, projectors or whiteboards for everyone to see.

3 Brainstorm the problem with guidelines

- Suspend judgement. Avoid negative evaluative comments such as 'that won't work' or 'that sounds silly'. Laugh with wild ideas, not at them.

- Accept that there may be a level of cynicism and lack of enthusiasm among participants. Bets, competitions and prizes can be used to counteract this.

- Consider using the following to generate further ideas:
  - call for a one-minute break, asking the group to look over ideas already noted before starting the flow again
  - offer a target, e.g. 'we just need six more to make fifty ideas!'
  - reflect and concentrate on one idea, e.g. 'how many ways are there to do this?'
  - look back at the restatements to pursue other lines of enquiry.

- Freewheel. Encourage (within limits) drifting or dreaming. Try to bring the subconscious into play. The wilder the idea, the better.

- Go for quantity not quality – the more the merrier. Suspend judgement for the time being. Evaluation will come later.

- Cross-fertilise. Pick up someone else's idea and suggest others leading from it.

- Encourage the group to choose a really wild and apparently senseless idea from the lists and generate ideas based on or arising from it.

4 Closure

Give a warning about five minutes from the end of the session. Participants will want to know what happens next. Explain that the lists will be circulated and do this within 24 hours, if possible, to retain freshness and familiarity. Provide contact details or a way of submitting additional ideas or further background information after the session and set a deadline for doing this. You may find that some participants have their best ideas after the session, when they have had time to think about it.

Inform participants that they will be notified of the ideas chosen or recommended for further action. Ask one last time for any comments, ideas or further thinking and thank members of the group for taking part.

Action checklist: evaluation

1 Get the team to scrutinise all the ideas to pick out any instant winners

Rank ideas giving three points for those that stand out, two for those that have possibilities and one for those that appear unsound, require too many resources, or do not meet the original objectives.

2 Reduce the number of 'twos' to a minimum

To reduce the number of ideas rated as 'two', apply criteria such as cost and acceptability, and consider whether the timescale is appropriate.

3 Apply 'reverse brainstorming' to the ideas

- In how many ways can a particular idea fail?
- What are the negative factors?
- What is the potential downside for the organisation?

4 Apply the key evaluative criteria

- What will it cost?
- Will it be acceptable to management, staff and customers?
- Is it legal?
- Is it practical?
- How long will it take?
- How easy will it be to implement?
- What competition will there be?

● How time-sensitive or urgent is it? (If it is not done now, will an opportunity be lost?)

While the main brainstorming session should be free of negativity, there is a need for critique and evaluation at this stage to make the session constructive and useful. Brainstorming should ultimately provide solutions that are both original and workable, rather than a stream of unfeasible suggestions.

As a manager you should avoid:

● allowing unconstructive critical comments

● letting the session be dictated or sidetracked by dominant individuals

● letting the session go on too long

● recording the whole session

● allowing the session to be used to get buy-in for an existing idea.

Making rational decisions

Decision-making is the process of choosing between alternative courses of action. It may take place at an individual or organisational level

This checklist provides an outline for making rational decisions and includes a simple decision-making framework. It is therefore relevant to all managers.

The nature of the decision-making process is influenced by an organisation's culture and structure, and a number of theoretical models have been developed. One well-known method for individual decision-making was developed by Charles Kepner and Benjamin Tregoe in their book *The New Rational Manager*, published in 1981. Specific techniques used in decision-making include heuristics and decision trees. Computer systems designed to assist managerial decision-making are known as decision support systems.

The rational model for decision-making:

- provides evidence and support for how the decision was made
- is particularly suitable for complex or fuzzy situations
- is thorough and systematic
- relies on effective information-gathering, rather than preconceived ideas
- is an effective technique for determining a course of action and securing commitment to it.

It is worth noting that information-gathering should not be confused with facts. A key feature of successful decision-making is that you identify preconceptions and assumptions, ask why they exist and what their use is, and treat them as valuable information.

There can, however, be drawbacks because the method:

- can be time-consuming and resource-intensive, especially in fast-moving situations
- relies heavily on information that may prove difficult to gather
- requires fairly strict adherence if the outcome is to be a rational decision
- highlights the possibility that a rational decision may not be the right one.

It is extremely useful and rational behaviour for managers not to ignore their gut feelings. But it is important to note that this is not equivalent to acting on those feelings.

Action checklist

1 Define the decision to be made

Be clear about the exact decision to make. This first step helps to clarify thinking, aids communications and provides a record for the future. It may lead to the discovery that assumptions have been made previously which have muddied the water.

For example, a decision needs to be made on which computer to buy.

2 Establish the objectives

The objectives (which are different from goals) are things that are desired from the decision and should be measurable wherever possible. At this stage it is not necessary to worry about any apparent incompatibilities between the objectives. This stage involves consultation, information seeking and checking, including establishing all the stakeholders who have an interest/ objective in the matter.

Your objectives may be: a computer which can access the internet anywhere, run CD-ROMs and DVDs and do word-processing, spreadsheets and graphics; has a large hard drive; and is affordable. So it must have: wireless internet access, USB ports, a CD-ROM/DVD drive, adequate RAM, a large hard drive and standard software packages and be within budget.

3 Classify the objectives

Differentiate between the essential (the 'musts') and the desirable (the 'wants') requirements. The fundamental difference between musts and wants is that if one of the decision alternatives does not meet a must, that option should be rejected. Failure to meet a want should not mean automatic rejection. The process for considering wants is dealt with in point 5.

● Musts: maximum price, minimum RAM memory capacity, minimum hard-drive capacity

● Wants: wireless internet, CD-ROM/DVD drive, USB ports, software packages

4 Define the 'musts'

To be a valid must, an objective should have a quantitative measure or an objective standard. Assign quantitative measures to the musts: maximum price £600; minimum 1GB RAM memory; minimum 100GB hard drive. This means that if an option presented for purchase is either over £600 or less than 1GB RAM, or has less than a 100GB hard drive, it should be rejected.

5 Define the 'wants'

Examine the wants for importance and give a numerical weighting out of 10 (10 for the most important, less than 10 for something less important). For example, if the software packages are the most important feature after the musts, software would be weighted 10. If an option includes spreadsheet, database, graphics and word-processing, it may well score 10 out of 10; if one is missing, it might score only 8. An extremely fast modem with built-in error correction may have a weight of 10; an option with a modem not so fast or sophisticated may score only 6 out of 10.

Wireless internet	10
Complete software package	10
Inbuilt CD-ROM/DVD	9
Extra USB ports	8

6 Generate the alternatives

With information requirements established, next seek and obtain the appropriate information. In this case sources may include PC suppliers, the trade press and informed colleagues.

7 Apply the alternatives to the requirements

The information – or options obtained – should be recorded for each alternative against each must objective.

8 Test the alternatives against the 'musts'

Reject those options that do not meet the musts. Do any of them not match against the musts on price, storage or processor? If negative, it is logical to reject that option.

If you do not wish it or something else prevents rejection of an option that has failed on musts, the musts are either proving unsatisfactory or you are not adhering to the rational process. In either case you should restart at point 3.

9 Score the remaining alternatives against the 'wants'

Score the remaining options against each of the wants in turn. The one that meets the want best should be scored highest and others allocated proportionate scores. For example:

Wireless internet	6
2 out of 4 software elements missing	5
No CD-ROM/DVD drive	0
2 extra memory slots	8

10 Multiply the weights by the scores

Weights should be multiplied by scores and the results added for each alternative. For example, as in points 5 and 9 above:

Wireless internet	10 x 6	60
2 out 4 software elements missing	10 x 5	50
No CD-ROM/DVD	9 x 0	0
2 extra memory slots	8 x 8	64
Total		174

11 Come to a provisional decision

The totals will enable you to come to a provisional decision. With the totals compared it is usually possible to make statements such as:

● option A is clearly the best

● options D and E are not worth considering

● there is little to choose between options B and C.

12 The final decision

The analysis will not provide an automatic decision, unless all options but one fail to meet the musts. Where several options have similar totals, it is particularly important to re-examine scores and weights and the evidence on which they are based. The analysis will provide a sound framework for clear examination. It is not always necessary to use the entire process described above, especially for simple binary (yes/no) decisions. However, each element in the process can be used separately to improve the efficiency of a decision. Some initial assumptions have to be made in the decision process. Make sure you review all the assumptions before proceeding to the analysis described above. In the computer example, a technological assumption we make at the beginning is that we need 4MB RAM maximum. Once the assumption is made, it will condition our choice and we need to be sure the assumption is correct.

As a manager you should avoid:

- jumping too quickly to an apparently obvious decision
- letting a preconceived notion influence the process
- cutting corners, especially if the decision has far-reaching implications
- letting personal preferences cloud the process
- taking the provisional decision as final
- ignoring your instinct
- using this approach for solving problems.

A simple decision-making framework

For less complex decisions or when qualitative data are considered, you can use the following table.

Desired result		
Possible solution #1	Pros	Cons
Possible solution #2	Pros	Cons
Possible solution #3	Pros	Cons
Recommendation and rationale		

Introducing performance measurement

A performance measurement system is an organised means of defining measures of performance and gathering, recording and analysing information to monitor performance against objectives, identify areas for improvement and take action to improve performance as necessary.

A key performance indicator (KPI) is a measure against which the management of any activity can be assessed. Measurement against the indicator enables managers to assess how efficiently, effectively or cost-effectively the operation is performing.

Performance measures provide a quantitative answer to whether you are reaching or exceeding targets. They require the collection of raw data and conversion through a formula into a numerical unit. For example, a target may have been set to reduce the proportion of customer complaints from 10% of total sales to 5% (the indicator). A formula to see whether this has been achieved would look like this:

$$\frac{\text{total number of complaints}}{\text{total number of sales}} \times 100 = \% \text{ of complaints}$$

Performance measures are used to assist in tracking organisational performance against objectives. Any system of performance measurement must be fully aligned with the organisational mission, strategy and values, and be integrated into the overall system of performance management that sets and monitors the achievement of organisational, departmental, team and individual objectives.

To evaluate the performance of an organisation or department, credible and reliable measures need to be in place. This checklist provides some principles to help managers introduce or improve performance measurement in their organisation and considers such questions as what to measure, how to measure it, what targets to set, how to gather, record and analyse performance information, and how to take action on the results.

Effective performance measurement can identify areas for improvement, help to keep performance on track, alert the organisation to potential threats, and enable managers to make decisions based on reliable results rather than instinct. Meaningful and actionable data can be a powerful tool for influencing behaviour and keeping one step ahead of the competition. To establish a successful performance measurement, processes, time, resources and planning are required.

Measuring performance has many advantages and enables an organisation to:

- understand the current position
- predict future financial performance
- maintain a record of historical performance
- identify strengths and weaknesses
- determine whether improvements have actually taken place
- establish a programme to benchmark against competitors, other organisations or previous results.

The financial measures traditionally used as a means of performance accounting are now more commonly balanced with non-financial measures, such as customer satisfaction and on-time delivery, to gain a more rounded picture of overall performance.

Action checklist

1 Designate those responsible for the performance measurement system

This should include members drawn from all levels and departments of the organisation who will be responsible for the design, implementation, management and review of performance measures. Appoint a coordinator (someone with project management experience who commands respect and can get things done) to oversee the system.

2 Ensure the support of employees

Senior management must fully support the system from the outset. Without their support it will be more difficult to instigate change and influence decision-making based upon the results of the measures.

It is equally important to win the support and cooperation of all other employees. Achieve this by explaining clearly why a performance measurement system is being introduced. Highlight the benefits that effective performance measurement will bring, emphasising it as a positive exercise. Be prepared for a negative reaction from employees who may view it as a form of personal monitoring. Allay anxiety by communicating the process clearly, openly and honestly, gaining buy-in from its inception. Provide an opportunity for employees to raise any concerns they may have.

3 Identify the activities to be measured

The selection of the right measures is crucial, as the relevance of the results will depend on what is measured.

Questions that should be considered when deciding what and how to measure performance include:

- What products or services do we provide?
- Who are our customers and stakeholders (internal and external)?
- What do we do?

- How do we do it?

  Think about the activities that contribute to the achievement of organisational goals and are essential for success. Resist the temptation to focus solely on measures where you know that the organisation will score highly.

  The number of activities to be measured will vary, but as a guide the key performance areas typically cover financial, market, environment, operations, people and adaptability. Avoid measuring too many activities for the sake of it – this will simply create an overwhelming set of results that will cause confusion and be difficult to analyse and act upon. It is helpful to place activities in order of priority to ensure that the main drivers of success are acted upon first.

4 Establish key performance indicators

Once the activities have been defined it is necessary to identify what information is required in relation to each one. What does success look like and what level of performance needs to be achieved? Which indicators will best reflect the key success factors? For each of the critical activities selected for measurement, it is necessary to establish a key performance indicator (KPI).

Good performance indicators are:

- realistic – they do not require unreasonable effort to meet
- understandable – they should be expressed in simple and clear terms
- adaptable – they can be changed if conditions change
- economic – the cost of setting and administering should be low in relation to the activity covered
- legitimate – they should be in line with or exceed legislative requirements
- measurable – they should be communicable with precision.

A period of observation may be appropriate if it is the first time an indicator is to be established for an activity. Similar organisations may be prepared to offer information on the targets they set; this can then be used to establish your own indicators. From the performance indicator you will be able to identify what data need to be collected.

5 Provide a balanced set of measures

Linking measures to key success factors is critical to effective performance measurement, and introducing a balance of financial and non-financial measures offers the flexibility to achieve this. A company's success is often judged by how it performs financially, so traditional financial measures are valuable for senior managers and external stakeholders. However, many performance aspects, such as customer satisfaction, product quality and delivery times, simply cannot be captured by financial measures alone. For many employees, operational and non-financial measures are more easily aligned with personal objectives, and thus help in gaining valuable employee support for performance measurement. Use both forms of measurement to get a complete picture of overall performance.

6 Collect the data

Once the measures have been decided and agreed, the next step is to determine how the data will be collected and by whom. Ask yourself:

- What am I trying to measure?
- Where will I make the measurement?
- How accurate and precise must the measurements be?
- How often do I need to take the measurement?

For activities that are undertaken frequently it may be feasible for only a sample measure to be taken, say at every eighth event. In many cases the data required for the performance measurement will already exist, for example in databases or log books. There will be instances where an automated data collection system can or should be installed to provide accurate data without the need for human intervention.

As appropriate, inform individuals when they should start collecting data and in what format it should be presented: graphs, tables, datasheets or spreadsheets, and so on. All the data should be passed on to those responsible for analysis.

7 Implement the system with care

Introducing and launching new performance measures is a major operation. Adequate time and resources need to be available in advance to ensure a smooth launch and minimise disruption. Communicate the timescale for implementation widely and make sure that everyone is fully aware of its intended format and use. Carrying out a pilot or 'soft' launch will help you identify any potential problems.

8 Analyse the data

Before drawing conclusions from the data, verify that:

- the data appear to answer the questions that were originally asked
- there is no evidence of bias in the collection process
- there is enough data to draw meaningful conclusions.

Once the data have been verified the required performance measurement can be formulated. This may involve the use of a computer spreadsheet if there is a large amount of data. The results of the performance measures should be compared with the indicator set for each activity.

9 Consider whether the indicators need to be adjusted

Once the indicators have been analysed the following may be observed:

- the activity is underperforming – the indicator should be left as it is, but the reasons for failure should be identified and action taken to remedy the situation

- variance is not significant – a higher indicator should be set to achieve continuous improvement

- the indicator is easily achieved – if indicators are not challenging, continuous improvement is unlikely to be encouraged.

Consider how to adjust the indicators in order to gather meaningful data and put the necessary amendments in place.

10 Communicate the results

Summarise the data and prepare a report by following these steps:

- categorise the data and use graphs to show trends

- make the report comparative to goals or standards

- make sure all performance measurements start and end in the same month or year

- adopt a standard format by using the same size sheets and charts

- add basic conclusions.

Share the findings of the report widely both with internal employees and external stakeholders. Do not be tempted to gloss over negative results or, worse still, ignore them. Communication needs to be consistent, timely, accurate and unbiased. Only then will performance measurement become credible and useful.

Choose the most appropriate communication channel to suit the audience – email, intranet, newsletter, or formal presentation or meeting. Consider communicating positive results to suppliers or customers too as a means of promotion – for example, that 99% of customers rate the products as excellent. It may be beneficial to follow up the distribution of data with a workshop to make sure that everyone understands the implications of the results.

11 Take action

Identify areas for improvement and consider what steps may be needed to achieve improvements. Negative results may raise awareness of issues that may have been largely unknown, or confirm what was suspected. Positive results can also be used to make further improvements. Even good practice can be improved upon, so avoid complacency and utilise the results to continue to make innovative improvements. Discuss the need for changes with relevant individuals, assign responsibility for action and monitor recommended improvements. Equip employees with the tools and resources required, and consider whether training or development are needed.

12 Continue to measure performance and evaluate performance measures

The process of collecting data and analysing performance should be continuous. Goals and standards should be increased as performance improves, or adjusted as activities change. Measures will only be relevant for as long as the activity being measured remains the same. Aim to review each set of measures at least annually to ensure that they remain relevant. Consistency in the testing and measurement of different activities will help to track performance over time.

As a manager you should avoid:

- failing to align performance measures with organisation strategy and objectives
- setting performance measures in stone – modify them as processes and activities change
- failing to act on the results of performance measurement
- underestimating the resources (staff and time) that measuring performance will consume
- introducing too many measures.

Implementing the balanced scorecard

The balanced scorecard is defined as a strategic management and measurement system that links strategic objectives to comprehensive indicators. The key to the success of the system is that it must be a unified, integrated set of indicators that measure the activities and processes at the core of an organisation's operating environment.

The balanced scorecard takes into account not only the traditional 'hard' financial measures but also three categories of 'soft' quantifiable operational measures:

- **financial perspective** – timely and accurate financial data are essential

- **customer perspective** – how an organisation is perceived by its customers

- **internal perspective** – areas in which an organisation must excel through business process improvements

- **innovation, learning and growth perspective** – supported by knowledge management activities and initiatives, areas in which an organisation must improve and add value to its products, services, or operations.

Measurements taken across these four categories are seen to provide a rounded balanced scorecard that reflects organisational performance more accurately than one based solely on financial indicators. This in turn assists managers to focus on their mission, rather than merely on short-term financial gain. It also helps to motivate staff to achieve strategic objectives.

Traditionally, managers have used a series of indicators to measure how well their organisations are performing. These measures relate essentially to financial aspects such as business ratios, productivity, unit costs, growth and profitability. While useful in themselves, they provide only a narrowly focused snapshot of how an organisation performed in the past and give little indication of likely future performance.

During the early 1980s, the rapidly changing business environment prompted managers to take a broader view of performance. Consequently, a range of other factors started to be taken into account, exemplified by the McKinsey 7-S model and popularised by Tom Peters and Robert Waterman's book, *In Search of Excellence*. These provide a broader assessment of corporate health in both the immediate and the longer term. This checklist focuses on the balanced scorecard, which was developed by Robert Kaplan and David Norton in the early 1990s with the aim of providing a balanced view of an organisation's performance.

The balanced scorecard has become an increasingly popular performance management and measurement framework and regularly appears in the top ten in Bain & Company's most used annual management tools surveys.

Kaplan and Norton identified a number of stages for implementing the scorecard. These include a mix of planning, interviews, workshops and reviews. The type, size and structure of an organisation will determine the detail of the implementation process and the number of stages adopted. This checklist outlines some of the main steps.

Action checklist

1 Be clear about organisational strategy and objectives

As the scorecard is inextricably linked to strategy, the first requirement is to clearly define the strategy and make sure that senior managers, in particular, are familiar with the key issues. Before any other action can be planned, it is essential to have an understanding of:

- the strategy
- the key objectives or goals required to realise the strategy
- the three or four critical success factors (CSFs) that are fundamental to the achievement of each major objective or goal.

Starting with strategy and objectives is crucial and will help organisations avoid doing the wrong things really well.

2 Develop a strategy map

Strategy mapping is a tool developed by Kaplan and Norton for translating strategy into operational terms. A strategy map provides a graphical representation of cause and effect between strategic objectives and shows how the organisation creates value for its customers and stakeholders. Generally, improving performance in the objectives under learning and growth enables the organisation to improve performance in its internal processes, which in turn enables it to create desirable results in the customer and financial perspectives.

3 Decide what to measure

Once the organisation's major strategic objectives have been determined, a set of measures can be developed. The measures chosen must reflect the strategic objectives and help to align action with strategy. As a guide, there should be a limit of 15–20 key measures linked to those specific goals (significantly fewer may not achieve a balanced view, and significantly more may become unwieldy and deal with non-critical issues).

Based on the four main perspectives suggested by Kaplan and Norton, a list of goals and measures may include some of the following:

Financial (shareholder) perspective

- **Goals** – increased profitability, growth, increased return on their investment
- **Measures** – cash flows, cost reduction, economic value added, gross margins, profitability, return on capital, equity, investments and sales, revenue growth, working capital, turnover

Customer perspective

- **Goals** – new customer acquisition, retention, extension, satisfaction
- **Measures** – market share, customer service, customer satisfaction, number of new, retained or lost customers, customer profitability, number of complaints, delivery times, quality performance, response time

Internal perspective

- **Goals** – improved core competencies, improved critical technologies, reduction in paperwork, better employee morale
- **Measures** – efficiency improvements, development, lead or cycle times, reduced unit costs, reduced waste, amount of recycled waste, improved sourcing/supplier delivery, employee morale and satisfaction, internal audit standards, number of employee suggestions, sales per employee, staff turnover

Innovation and learning perspective

- **Goals** – new product development, continuous improvement, employee development
- **Measures** – number of new products and percentage of sales from these, number of employees receiving training, training hours per employee, number of strategic skills acquired, alignment of personal goals with the scorecard

4 Amend the scorecard if appropriate

Each organisation must determine its own strategic goals and the activities to be measured. Some organisations have found that Kaplan and Norton's template fails to meet their particular needs and have either modified it or devised their own scorecard. Public-sector organisations, for example, may have different aims and objectives and may have to tailor the scorecard to reflect this.

One way to do this, to reflect the fact that people are a major cost item and also a major driver of value, is as follows:

- financial – as above
- customer – as above
- internal – concentrating on systems and processes
- people – focusing on leadership, learning and development, performance management, employee engagement etc.

5 Finalise the implementation plan

Further discussions, interviews and workshops may be required to fine-tune the detail and agree the strategy, goals and activities to be measured, ensuring that the measures selected focus on the critical success factors. At this stage, it is critical to be clear about what 'good' looks like.

It may be worth identifying the key business processes, and drawing up a matrix of key business processes and critical success factors. Key business processes that have an impact on many critical success factors should attract more attention and improvement efforts than those that influence few or no critical success factors.

Before implementation, targets, rates and other criteria must be set for each of the measures, and processes for how, when and why the measures are to be recorded should be put in place.

6 Implement the system

An implementation plan should be produced and the whole project communicated to employees. Everyone should be informed at the beginning of the project and kept up-to-date on progress. It is crucial to communicate clearly with employees. Explain the purpose and potential benefits of the system to them and make sure that everyone is aware that they have a role to play in achieving corporate goals. There should be a 'golden thread' linking personal objectives to organisational goals. Ideally, this will be achieved through an organisational performance management system.

The system for recording and monitoring the measures should be in place and tested well before the start date, and, as far as possible, training in its use should be given to all users. The system should automatically record all the data required, though some of the measurements may need to be input manually.

7 Publicise the results

The results of all measurements should be collated regularly: daily, weekly, monthly, quarterly, or as appropriate. This will potentially comprise a substantial amount of complex data, and you need to decide who will have access to the full data: senior management only, divisional or departmental heads, or all employees. Alternatively, partial information may be provided on a need-to-know basis. Decide how the results will be publicised – through meetings, newsletters, the organisation's intranet or any other appropriate communication channels.

8 Utilise the results

Any form of business appraisal is not an end in itself. It is a guide to organisational performance and may point to areas (management, operational, procedural) that require strengthening. Taking action based upon the obtained information is as important as the data itself. Indeed, management follow-up action should be seen as an essential part of the appraisal process.

9 Review and revise the system

After the first cycle has been completed, a review should be undertaken to assess the success, or otherwise, of both the information gathered and the action taken, in order to determine whether any part of the process requires modification.

Refrain from using the same scorecard measures year after year. Review the existing measures and, where appropriate, remove flawed measures and replace them with more reliable ones. Be prepared to introduce additional measures to reflect current circumstances, for example to measure an organisation's ethical performance.

As a manager you should avoid:

- setting measures that do not relate to critical success factors
- over-measuring the organisation
- allowing the measurement process to interfere with employees' ability to get on with the job
- adopting an off-the-shelf system not suited to the organisation.

Robert Kaplan and David Norton

The balanced scorecard

Introduction

Robert Kaplan (b. 1940) and David Norton (b. 1941) are jointly recognised as popularisers of the balanced scorecard and their approach to it was first introduced in a 1992 *Harvard Business Review* article, 'The Balanced Scorecard: Measures that Drive Performance'. Kaplan and Norton turned the popular saying 'What gets measured gets done' on its head and began with 'What you measure is what you get'.

Kaplan studied at MIT, where he gained a BS and an MS in electrical engineering, and then at Cornell University, where he gained a PhD in operations research. He then spent sixteen years on the faculty of Carnegie-Mellon University, serving as dean from 1977 to 1983. He moved on to Harvard Business School in 1984 and is now Baker Foundation Professor. Kaplan has received a number of awards and in 2006 he was elected to the Accounting Hall of Fame.

David Norton is a consultant, researcher and speaker in the field of strategic performance management. He is the founder and director of Palladium Group, a professional services firm focusing on performance measurement and management. Previously he worked at Renaissance Solutions, a consulting company that he co-founded with Kaplan in 1992, and at Nolan, Norton & Company, where he was president for sixteen years.

The balanced scorecard is an aid to developing and managing

strategy by looking at how key measures interrelate to track progress. Kaplan and Norton argue that adherence to quarterly financial returns and the bottom line alone will not provide organisations with an overall strategic view. The balanced scorecard, though, goes beyond the exploitation of financial measures alone by incorporating three other key perspectives:

- a customer perspective – which addresses how customers see the organisation
- an internal business perspective – which requires the organisation to identify that at which it needs to excel
- a learning/innovation perspective – which addresses what the organisation needs to improve to create value in the future.

By commenting on the present and indicating the drivers of the future, the scorecard both measures and motivates business performance.

Setting up the balanced scorecard

Kaplan and Norton argue that strategies often fail because they are not converted successfully into actions that employees can understand and apply in their everyday work. It is difficult to formulate realistic measures that are meaningful to those doing the work, relate visibly to strategic direction and provide a balanced picture of what is happening throughout the organisation, not just one facet of it. It is this aspect that the balanced scorecard addresses.

The balanced scorecard concentrates on measures in four strategic areas – finance, customers, internal business processes and learning and innovation – and requires the implementing organisation to identify goals and measures for each of them. For a detailed breakdown of these four areas, see the 'Implementing the balanced scorecard' checklist, page 182.

The scorecard provides a description of the organisation's strategy. It will indicate where problems lie because it shows the interrelationships between goals and linked activities. It creates an understanding of what is going on elsewhere in the organisation and shows all employees how they are contributing. Providing that accurate and timely information is fed into the system, it helps to focus attention on where change and learning are needed through the cause-and-effect relationships it can reveal. Examples of the types of insight achieved were detailed in *Linking the Balanced Scorecard to Strategy*:

If we increase employee training about products, then they will become more knowledgeable about the full range of products they can sell;

If employees are more knowledgeable about products, then their sales effectiveness will improve;

If their sales effectiveness improves, then the average margins of products they sell will increase.

Implementing the balanced scorecard

In *Putting the Balanced Scorecard to Work*, Kaplan and Norton identify eight steps towards building a scorecard:

1 **Preparation.** Select/define the strategy/business unit to which to apply the scorecard. Think in terms of the appropriateness of the four main perspectives defined above.

2 **First interviews.** Distribute information about the scorecard to senior managers along with the organisation's vision, mission and strategy. A facilitator will interview each manager on the organisation's strategic objectives and ask for initial thoughts on scorecard measures.

3 **First executive workshop.** Match measures to strategy. The management team is brought together to develop the scorecard. From agreeing the vision statement, the team debates each of the four key strategic areas, addressing the following questions:

● If my vision succeeds, how will I differ?

● What are the critical success factors?

- What are the critical measurements?

  These questions help to focus attention on the impact of turning the vision into reality and what to do to make it happen. It is important to represent the views of customers and shareholders and gain a number of measures for each critical success factor.

4 **Second interviews.** The facilitator reviews and consolidates the findings of the workshop and interviews each of the managers individually about the emerging scorecard.

5 **Second workshop.** Team debate on the proposed scorecard; the participants discuss the proposed measures, link ongoing change programmes to the measures, and set targets or rates of improvement for each of the measures. Start outlining the communication and implementation processes.

6 **Third workshop.** Final consensus on vision, goals, measures and targets. The team devises an implementation programme on communicating the scorecard to employees, integrating the scorecard into management philosophy, and developing an information system to support the scorecard.

7 **Implementation.** The implementation team links the measures to information support systems and databases and communicates the what, why, where and who of the scorecard throughout the organisation. The end-product should be a management information system which links strategy to the shop-floor activity.

8 **Periodic review.** Balanced scorecard measures can be prepared for review by senior management at appropriate intervals.

Since the publication of their first book on the balanced scorecard, Kaplan and Norton have continued to develop their ideas and clarify how they can be implemented to maximum effect. In *The Strategy-Focused Organization*, they looked at how companies were using the scorecard and identified five principles for translating strategy into operational terms and aligning management and measurement systems to organisational strategy. A third book, *Strategy Maps: Converting Intangible Assets into Intangible Outcomes*, introduced the concept of 'strategy maps', which provide a visual framework for describing how value is created within organisations from each of the four balanced scorecard perspectives. *Alignment: Using the Balanced Scorecard to Create Corporate Strategies* looks at how to align organisational business units to overall strategy and how to use a strategy map to clarify and communicate corporate priorities to all business units and their employees.

A later book, published in 2008, *The Execution Premium: Linking Strategies to Operations for Competitive Advantage*, explores this theme further, focusing on how to put strategy into action to achieve financial success.

In perspective

The balanced scorecard can be seen as the latest in a long line of attempts at management control, starting with F. W. Taylor and continuing through work measurement systems, quality assurance systems and performance indicators. Commentators suggest that the scorecard is flexible and can be adapted for use by individual organisations, and it is practical, straightforward and devoid of obscure theory. Most importantly, it responds to many organisations' requirements to expand strategically on traditional financial measures and points to areas for change. It is also used successfully in the public sector, where the focus is on organisational mission rather than financial return for shareholders.

The balanced scorecard has become increasingly popular. Bain & Company's 2007 survey of management tools suggests that 66% of companies are using it worldwide, with usage highest in Asia and in large companies.

However, the level of satisfaction with the tool has declined since the previous survey and is now below the average for the tools covered by the survey. In *The Design and Implementation of the Balanced Business Scorecard: an Analysis of Three Companies in Practice*, Stephen Letza suggests that it cannot be regarded as a panacea. He states that the balanced scorecard should highlight performance as a continuous, dynamic and integrated process, act as an integrating tool, function as the pivotal tool for an organisation's current and future direction, and deliver information that is the backbone of the strategy. He also highlights some of the major drawbacks in using the balanced scorecard and points out the need to:

- avoid being swamped by the minutiae of too many detailed measures and make sure that measures relate to the strategic goals of the organisation

- make sure that all activities are included – this ensures that everyone is contributing to the organisation's strategic goals

- watch out for conflict as information becomes accessible to those not formerly in a position to see it and try to harness conflict constructively.

Kaplan and Norton have attempted to ensure that the scorecard is used correctly through their provision of education and consultancy programmes and by establishing a Hall of Fame, which showcases companies that have successfully implemented the balanced scorecard.

Choosing a growth strategy

A growth strategy is a strategy by which an organisation aims to develop and expand its business and improve its profitability. Traditional growth strategies include market penetration, product development, market development and diversification.

Most companies have to grow in order to stay in business; and for this they need a strategy. Even those that do not plan to grow significantly in size still need to make carefully thought-through strategic choices. Change is inevitable and companies have to adapt, whether they wish to stay local or conquer the globe.

A company has big decisions to make as it grows. It needs to create space at the board level to have genuinely strategic discussions. Questions that need to be considered include:

- How big do we intend to go?
- In which regions of the world should we operate?
- Which technologies do we need to develop or acquire?
- How do we ensure that expansion is adequately resourced?
- What is our appetite for risk, and our approach to debt?

As well as addressing the scale and geography of growth, companies have to make big decisions on the way in which they grow. For example, will it be by building a large central organisation or through strategic partnerships or franchising?

The extent to which a company specialises in its core competence or diversifies is another big decision. Both involve significant risks, but there is considerable research and literature to guide managers.

Companies can be understood as going through stages or cycles of growth and different markets and sectors have their own cycles. There is much more dynamism, instability and change in younger areas like social media than in an established, mature market like automobiles. In the field of social media, a start-up can grow to become one of the largest companies in the world in just three or four years; whereas in a business such as aerospace, which involves large capital investments and lengthy product development times, this would not be possible. No sector is static, however; some markets can be relatively stable for decades and then be transformed within a few years through a disruptive technology.

Business schools and consultancies have developed many different models that have helped businesses understand what stage they are at in these cycles. These models can be followed too slavishly. It would be a mistake to assume that your business will follow a textbook model predictably – internal and external events will complicate the picture. A further important complication is that different parts of a business may be at different stages of a certain cycle.

However, it is probably more risky to ignore such cycles or phases of development completely. Many businesses struggle because they fail to adapt their style or depth of management through the growth phases, or as the business becomes larger. For example, entrepreneurs are often not the best people to manage routine business processes, such as finance or procurement, as the company grows. Successful business pioneers such as Richard Branson and Stelios Haji-Ioannou hire teams of professional managers and delegate day-to-day operations to them.

Any start-up that grows and begins to hire more people reaches a stage where no single individual can know every employee and personally manage the business. The firm needs to hire professional specialists and managers, not only for product development, customer service and marketing, but also in the essential support services such as finance and personnel. A company can go out of business if its tax returns are frequently late or employment law is not adhered to, even if the business and services are otherwise excellent. If a business becomes very large, specialist departments become entire divisions. These developments need to be carefully planned. There are choices to be made regarding the levels of integration and centralisation within large international companies, and the extent to which they are committed to working with external partners.

Growth is not necessarily about scale – it might be a matter of a greater emphasis on quality or profit margins, or a commitment to avoid acquisitions or high levels of debt. But these are also strategic decisions that require serious thought and discussion.

This checklist is divided into two sections:

- understanding the major growth strategy options
- selecting a practical course of action to follow.

Action checklist: understanding the major growth strategy options

1 Be clear about the type of growth you want

This may not simply be a matter of scale. Growth is not necessarily about becoming large or international, but a company does have to adapt and be dynamic in order to thrive. Growth in at least some dimensions will be necessary. A company may choose to stay local, like an independent store, or be global but niche, like an elite sports-car manufacturer, but this still involves a strategic choice. To be effective, such a strategy typically involves growth in some dimensions other than size – for example, quality, profit margins and prestige. If ambitious growth is planned, major decisions on which geographical regions and product ranges to focus on have to be made.

2 Focus versus diversification

Companies typically have a core specialism at which they truly excel. The discipline of core competence has been much discussed and researched. It suits many companies to concentrate on their main areas of expertise and work with suppliers and partners, rather than attempt to be expert in a wider range, but this approach can include some diversification into closely related areas. Working with specialist partners means that the company can remain more focused and not too bureaucratic or large; however, managing such external relationships still requires considerable attention and expertise in strategic relationship management. And bear in mind that new competitors and disruptive technologies can wreck an established business model in an area of core expertise, so some degree of diversification or adaptation may be unavoidable.

3 Centralisation versus decentralisation

If a company aims to become very large internationally, it has to make a decision about whether it will operate as a single entity or as a network of semi-independent entities. For example, will you seek economies of scale by introducing shared service centres for geographic regions, or will each business have its own back office? Would centralising a function have implications for the company's brand promise? For example, Pret A Manger, a sandwich chain, has sandwiches prepared locally, because the promise of fresh preparation is more important than economies of scale that might be achieved by centralisation. A related option is franchising, in which the owner of a brand hires individual local companies to operate as franchisees, running businesses following the brand owner's established operational approach.

4 Take technological developments into account

All companies need to be aware of technological developments in fields such as social media and 'big data', which may affect their business as they grow, whether or not the service they offer is technology-related. Business strategy and IT strategy cannot be considered in isolation; they must be looked at together to produce an integrated strategy for the business. Technological considerations are also important in the resourcing of the growth strategy.

5 Understand the cycles of development

Companies use several models to help understand the phases of organisational development. Some have been criticised for being too simple or formulaic, but the hazards are often in the implementation, rather than the design. Any model straightforward enough to be presented on a chart will be a simplification. As long as this is recognised, the model may still be useful. The point is to use it to generate deep discussions within the organisation that will give managers a clearer understanding of the phase that a company is entering and the strategic choices it faces.

Action checklist: selecting a growth strategy

1 Remember that change is inevitable and adaptation is always necessary

While growth in terms of scale is not inevitable, change is. The emergence of an unexpected competitor or a new disruptive technology may affect the core business. A business typically needs to be responsive to actual or potential threats and to constantly reinvent itself.

2 Analyse internal and external dynamics

An honest inquiry into a company's profile and context is a good first step. A standard SWOT analysis of strengths, weaknesses, opportunities and threats is often helpful. Some management teams go beyond a simple list under each heading and consider how well, for example, a strength matches an opportunity, mapping these out on a grid. A similar tool, more focused on external matters, is PEST or PESTLE analysis, which focuses on the political, economic, social, technological, legal and environmental factors affecting an organisation.

3 Create regular, deep discussions about growth strategy

The board and the senior management team need to set aside time for deep discussions about the major strategic decisions on growth and have these at regular intervals. There needs to be honest feedback on the extent to which strategy is being implemented, and, if there are failures and setbacks, discussion of how initiatives can be renewed or alternative strategies adopted. Continual monitoring is needed.

4 Nurture the established business as well as the innovations

An inappropriate use of the popular Boston matrix (see Growth models below) is to invest too much in 'stars' – potential future profit centres – and neglect established 'cash cows' or profit centres. Some brands, especially in fashion and food and drink, have long life spans that are measured in centuries, with an appeal to tradition. An example is Jack Daniel's, a premium whisky company, which has boasted in advertisements that it is not planning any improvements. Such brands may nonetheless require marketing investment. Although the product does not change, there may be a need for innovation and the use of new technology in promotions and customer relationships.

5 Allocate adequate resources for the growth strategy

Resourcing a growth strategy adequately is essential. Going global is not just a question of scaling up. Different countries vary enormously in cultural attitudes, ways of working, education levels, tax and employment law, and so on. Consumer tastes can vary considerably and so can the role of trade unions. Some countries may have skills shortages in disciplines that are needed for your growth strategy. The IT architecture also has to be planned at a strategic level and must be adequate to support a growing business.

6 Pay attention to communication, engagement and teamwork

Successful growth strategies depend at least as much on the how as on the what. Communication, engagement and sense of direction are as important as skill levels and getting the big decisions right. Managers should communicate clearly and frequently to ensure that everyone involved is aware of the strategic objectives and their role in making them happen, and is actively engaged with the process. Employee opinion surveys are useful in picking up indicators of both achievement and problems in this area. In the case of an acquisition, cultural fit is at least as important as strategic fit, and can be particularly challenging when entering a new geographical region.

7 Maintain culture and values as you grow

Many successful companies have clearly defined founding principles – relating, for example to honest conduct, customer service or teamwork. As an organisation grows, these must continue to be at the heart of the way it does business. Make sure that values are clearly articulated and written down, and that induction and training programmes are in place to instil them across the organisation. With a growing start-up, it is especially important to introduce these initiatives as the company becomes too large for the founder to know every employee.

8 Plan for continuity and succession

One challenge for ambitious, growth-oriented businesses is the recruitment and development of professional managers, including the CEO. Firms that intend to stay small or medium-sized, including many family firms or partnerships, have challenging decisions to make on succession: what happens when the founding partners, or siblings, die or retire? Such firms need to make long-term plans, and prepare for contingencies.

Growth models

Boston matrix. A simple 2 × 2 matrix that categorises products or businesses as 'stars' (high potential), 'cash cows' (mature profitable businesses), 'dogs' (small market share in mature market) and 'question marks' (uncertainty with regard to viability).

Ansoff matrix. Used to help understand the difference between new products with an existing market, such as brand extensions; new markets with an existing product, such as new geographies; and genuine diversification – a new product and new market.

Greiner's five stages. First developed in the early 1970s by Larry Greiner, and revised in the late 1990s, this model describes the phases of company growth and development and identifies the managerial challenge at each stage. The five stages are creativity; direction; delegation; coordination; collaboration. Greiner later suggested a sixth stage, relating to extra-organisational relationships.

Churchill's five phases. First produced in 1983 by Neil Churchill of INSEAD. The five phases are existence; survival; success; take-off; resource-maturity.

Adizes model. A living organism metaphor, developed by Ichak Adizes. This describes the company as going through birth, adolescence, maturity, prime, and so on.

The DIAMOND model. Developed by BDO Stoy Hayward, this stands for dreaming up the idea; initiating the business plan; attacking problems of growth; maturing; overhauling the business; networking; diversifying.

Three Horizons. Developed by McKinsey consultants, the horizons are the business core; a newer line of business activity; experimentation.

As a manager you should avoid:

● assuming that you don't need a growth strategy because you don't plan to become very large or international

- thinking that styles of management or company structure don't need to change as the company grows
- neglecting cultural differences when working in new regions
- expanding sales too far without sufficient support and resourcing
- treating communication and engagement as the 'soft stuff' or an optional extra.

Mergers and acquisitions

The distinction between the terms 'merger' and 'acquisition' is becoming increasingly blurred in common usage. In many situations they are treated as one and the same, but there are important differences.

An acquisition is where one business acquires another by gaining ownership of its net assets or liabilities. This may be welcomed by the acquired company or it may be heavily contested, resulting in acrimonious and public disputes.

A merger is often an agreed union of one or more organisations. A merger can be the result of a friendly takeover that results in the combining of companies on an equal footing. After a merger, the legal existence of the acquired organisation is terminated. The degree of friendliness in such unions can, however, vary considerably.

In reality, there is no standard template of a merger, as each union is different, depending on what is expected from the merger, and on the negotiations, strategy, stock and assets, human resources and shareholders of the players.

However, three broad types of merger are recognised:

- **horizontal merger** – involves firms from the same industry, operating at the same points in the supply chain
- **vertical merger** – involves firms from different points in the supply chain in the same industry
- **conglomerate merger** – a union of firms with few or no

similarities in production or marketing that come together to create a larger economic base and greater profit potential.

A merger is different from a consolidation, a joint venture, or a partnership.

Mergers and acquisitions (M&A) are an integral part of the business landscape and a valuable tool for business growth. They form part of the strategy of many businesses across a number of sectors – in the online sector, for example, being acquired soon after creation is almost a benchmark of success.

M&A may be undertaken for various reasons:

- strategic – with the aim of increasing market share, for example
- financial – where a cash-rich business buys an undervalued business
- organisational or personal – where the ambitions of a board drive the process.

It should be noted that the M&A process can take a long time to complete, may need the input of many outside specialists and advisers, and may require the lengthy commitment of a high-level internal team. Even with this input, many mergers or acquisitions are not completed or fail to deliver the expected returns.

Managers should understand that the M&A process needs to be focused and strategically driven. There is a need to look for untapped value, but also to give consideration to strategic and cultural fit. There is also a greater recognition of the need to engage with all stakeholders in the process, including the employees, customers and shareholders of all the businesses involved.

M&A framework

It is widely contended that each merger or acquisition is different, but broadly all deals follow a similar pattern or set of steps:

- Strategy development: determine if M&A is an appropriate approach

- Prepare the organisation and project team for the M&A
- Determine a shortlist or single target and investigate pricing and valuation; commence post-merger integration planning
- Commence negotiations between both sets of managers
- Structure the deal: complete due diligence; arrange financing; seek approval from stakeholders
- Close the deal
- Integrate the two organisations
- Review and evaluate the success of the M&A process

Elements of this framework will be addressed in this checklist.

Action checklist

1 Be aware of where you are and where you want to go

Every organisation should know what it is aiming to achieve, why and how it should do it, and where it is going in the future. Strategic planning addresses a number of basic questions:

- Where are you now?
- How did you get there?
- What business are you in, or should you be in?
- Where do you want to be in the future?
- How are you going to get there?
- What do you need to do to get there?

You should consider undertaking a SWOT analysis as a way of evaluating your strengths and weaknesses. This allows you to assess internal capabilities and resources that are under organisational control and external factors that are not under organisational control. This knowledge will help you develop your growth strategy and see where the opportunities lie.

2 Review your growth strategy

There are three main routes to growth for businesses: organic growth; joint ventures or partnerships; and mergers and acquisitions. All businesses should be exploring organic growth options as a cost-efficient way of expanding, but many will be looking at all three options. Before initiating a merger or acquisition you should consider whether your organisation has:

- the funds to support this approach
- the appropriate skills and capabilities among its senior management team.

Why you are seeking to expand and in what way? Do you want to:

- gain a greater market share
- extend your product range or customer base
- fill a gap in your technical capabilities or knowledge
- move out of one product range or sector into another
- reduce your costs and overheads
- develop your distribution channels?

3 Decide whether an acquisition will help you achieve your strategic objectives

Once you have established your strategic objectives you need to consider where M&A fits into this process. Like all other strategic decisions M&A should aim to deliver added value. The adoption of such an approach to growth should be justified on the grounds of cost and relative benefit, and should not be decided on the personal preference of members of the senior management team. There are various tools and models to help you determine the effectiveness of your approach, including the Boston matrix, Ansoff's product-market matrix and Porter's five forces.

Is a merger the best way to deliver your aims? Can you deliver these through organic growth of your existing business? Is working in partnership with another organisation a more cost-effective approach for your business?

An acquisition may not be the best or easiest approach and you need to be aware of all your options.

4 Appoint a senior project team

Senior managers play a key role in achieving M&A success. A large organisational merger will become the main focus of activity for the board both before and after the closure of the deal. In a merger of a smaller business a project team may be established.

Evaluate the skill set of the team and bring in appropriate external advisers as required. Identify the key roles and allocate responsibilities. Make sure the main areas are covered: intelligence gathering, managing finance, communicating and public relations, negotiating, engaging with stakeholders and integration planning

5 Identify possible targets

Your strategic review should provide the basic data to start the search for targets. Using this information you should be able to create a profile of a target company. Your profile should list all the desired features and possibly give some weighting to each. The list of features will vary depending upon your strategic objectives, but may include:

- type of activity
- size of company
- market position
- number and structure of employees
- product range
- production facilities
- supply chain
- structure of assets and equity
- profitability.

If you are looking to remain within the same sector, you should already have a strong working knowledge of who else is operating in the industry and what their strengths and weaknesses are. Knowledge of a company or some of its people is the most common way of finding a potential target. More often than not, the main source of target businesses is current competitors, suppliers or distributors. However, be prepared to take a wider view. Reflect upon your strategic objectives and think about whether a business outside your sector may be better placed to meet your needs.

6 Undertake valuations

Determining the value of a target business is a critical element of the merger process. Get the valuation wrong and you either end up paying too much for the business or find that you are unable to realise the expected value from the merger.

A business will have different values to different buyers depending on what they intend to use it for and the return they will obtain from it. This valuation may be different from the value placed on a business when winding up, for example. Buyers and sellers use the economic value of a business to determine the price at which they are prepared to buy or sell it. Business valuations are also used for estate, taxation and a number of other legal purposes. So before a valuation can be undertaken it is necessary to understand the reasons for the valuation – scrap value is generally worth less than going concern value.

If known, a value may take account of the price a willing buyer and a willing seller agree to. This is called the fair market value (FMV). However, the market conditions during this exchange might not have been perfect. Because markets are rarely perfect, a business valuation will usually start with a contextual evaluation of the economic and industry conditions surrounding the business. For example, is it a buoyant market or is it a market in recession? For a more accurate valuation, a business's financial performance and strength should be compared with that of others in the industry. Competitor valuations should also be considered.

Approaches to an initial business valuation include:

- asset valuations as a going concern
- income/earnings valuations as a going concern
- break-up asset valuations
- market valuations as a going concern.

The method used will depend upon the use the buyer has for the business, and each of these approaches will relate to a particular reason for selling or buying. It is common for a business to be valued on several bases and the differences between the resulting valuations explained.

7 Engage with the target's management teams

In an agreed merger it is advisable for the two sets of managements to get to know each other and to agree common objectives. A good approach is to get both management teams to spend some time together. This enables each team to learn about the other and to understand each other's position. Good sense and mutual respect will allow fruitful discussions about the way forward. This is not the place for large egos. Entrenched positions established at the start of the process get in the way of stakeholder interests.

Differences will emerge at some point. These may be:

- **strategic** – where the management teams start from wholly different base positions and understanding of the direction in which the business should move
- **cultural** – where businesses with very different backgrounds are trying to come together.

It is important that the management teams come together to work through these issues. The merged organisations will thrive only if there is agreement on strategic direction and how the organisations will develop together. It is possible that the culture of one organisation will dominate, but more commonly the culture of the new organisation is different from that of both the component organisations.

8 Structure the deal and complete due diligence

Due diligence is the term used to cover a variety of activities when researching another business. It should be viewed as an aid to understanding the business being bought, its business model, its market and its prospects.

Due diligence should aim to:

- verify assets and liabilities
- quantify risk
- identify growth potential and the benefits of merging
- provide a strong input into post-acquisition planning.

The list of topics which could be covered by due diligence is extensive. Consider the following broad areas as a starter:

- Cash flow
- Corporate governance compliance
- Directors and the senior team
- Environmental
- Finance and accounting
  - cash flow
  - debts
  - taxation
  - trading results
  - working capital
- Human resources
- Intellectual property
- IT and systems
- Legal disputes and litigation
- Markets and competitors
- Product information
- Property

- Research and development
- Shares and stakeholders
- Supply chains

  If you work for a larger organisation, you may find that you have the appropriate skills internally to complete due diligence. Smaller organisations will need to bring in expertise to complete the process. Investment in this area is cheap in comparison to litigation or the failure of the merger, which could have a serious long-term impact on both organisations.

9 Engage with stakeholders and plan for integration

Uncertainty among staff can have a huge negative impact on both organisations. Equally, the success of any merger will depend on the staff you bring with you into the new organisation. People often associate a merger with job losses and redundancy and so become resistant to any proposals for change. A managed approach to news releases, presenting common ground and agreed timescales, helps alleviate possible anxiety among stakeholders. Engage with people across both organisations. Be prepared to walk the shop floor. Treat people fairly, while recognising that there will be winners and losers.

You need to be prepared to move quickly once a deal has been struck. Develop plans for:

- taking financial control of the new organisation – effective cash management should receive particular attention
- making key appointments – prepare people to fill all the key positions in the new management team
- integrating operational, financial and IT systems
- focusing on value creation and the drivers for competitive advantage.

10 Avoid common reasons for deal failure

There has been a great deal of research and comment on why so many mergers and acquisitions fail, and the reasons for failure are wide and varied. Here are just a few of the potential pitfalls:

- Inappropriate or obsolete strategy – your strategy rationale is plainly wrong for your sector or for where you are as a business.

- Poor resourcing of the project team and a lack of understanding of the time it can take to free up staff for the team and fill their positions to ensure continuity of business.

- Rushed due diligence – either as a failure to allocate appropriate resources or by not understanding the full range of issues that need to be addressed.

- Failing to get to grips with the financials, through either poor valuations or missing some significant financial liability.

- Poor senior team management and governance – a clear decision-making process and clarity about who is able to make those decisions is needed to keep the project on track.

- Conflict and power struggles – either within the merger team or between the management teams of the two businesses.

- Incompatible IT systems or escalating costs when resolving IT systems issues.

- Weak leadership and a lack of courage when integrating the two businesses – tough decisions have to be made and a delay in making them only adds to uncertainty. Leaders need to demonstrate clarity, energy and enthusiasm and adopt behaviour that demonstrates the vision and culture of the new organisation.

- Poorly planned and executed integration – insufficiently detailed implementation plans, a failure to identify key interdependencies and a lack of focus on creating value.

A merger needs to be recognised as a significant change project, and as a manager you will need a significant amount of energy and resolution to see it through to a successful conclusion.

As a manager you should avoid:

- thinking that previous successful mergers will guarantee success with the next one
- failing to deliver the promised gains to shareholders
- pursuing deals for purely personal reasons
- continuing with a deal even when it is making no business sense
- thinking the work is done once the deal has been struck
- letting merger activity distract from current business operations and performance.

Strategic partnering

A strategic partnership or alliance is an agreement between two or more organisations to cooperate in a specific business activity to take joint advantage of market opportunities or to respond to customers more effectively than any of the partners could achieve individually. This involves the sharing of knowledge and expertise between partners as well as the reduction of risk and costs in areas such as relationships with suppliers and the development of new products and technologies. Such agreements may be for defined periods of time, and may be non-exclusive.

Partnering means:

- sharing risk and benefits with others and trusting them to act in joint best interests
- a strategic fit between partners so that objectives match and action plans show synergy
- finding complementary skills, competences and resources in partners
- sharing information which may have been privileged or confidential.

The development of new technologies, the globalisation of markets and the intensity of competition mean that the survival of single businesses is constantly under threat. There is a view that networks of autonomous companies are the way of the future. The development of the internet and associated technologies has facilitated closer collaboration across international borders, and the introduction of business-to-business IT platforms has enabled the sharing of commercially sensitive information between partners and even competitors. Partnering, as a collective term for various forms of inter-firm cooperation, including strategic alliances and collaborative projects, is an increasingly important theme and has become a way of life for many businesses.

Reasons for partnering include:

- gaining quicker, lower-risk access to new markets
- finding an outlet for excess capacity
- speeding up innovation, new product development, manufacture, launch and distribution
- reducing costs
- economies of scale through high volume, low cost and mass distribution
- integrating the supply chain
- strengthening the technological base
- sharing scarce resources
- overcoming geographic, legal or trade barriers
- for public-sector projects, benefiting from private-sector input.

Obstacles to successful partnering include:

- strategic fit between partners may be challenging, and organisational cultures and management styles may differ
- partners may lack a clear common goal
- partners may have differing or conflicting goals, cost expectations and timescales
- as a result of a poor selection process, one partner may emerge stronger than the other, creating an imbalance
- as a result of poor due diligence processes, one of the partners may not be able to fulfil their obligations under the partnership
- partners may fail to take account of cross-cultural issues in the integration process

- failure to develop relationships of trust
- inadequate communication – communication is key to overcoming cultural issues for example
- difference in leadership styles may cause implementation problems
- fuzzy communication and unclear reporting may lead to confusion, inter-partnership politics and a lack of trust and confidence
- decision-making may slow down because of the need to refer back to headquarters.

This checklist outlines the three planning phases of partnering: taking the strategic decision; structuring the strategic partnership; selecting the appropriate partner. The principles described apply equally to commercial partnerships, collaborative arrangements in the public sector and public/private-sector partnerships.

Action checklist: taking the strategic decision

1 Think carefully about partnering needs

Few organisations have all the resources or skills to tackle new market opportunities or other initiatives independently and maintain the economies of scale of low cost and high volume for mass distribution. Going it alone can mean high investment, a slower response to changing circumstances and the development of infrastructure that may require dismantling, possibly shortly afterwards. Conversely, partnering may mean sacrificing something unique and hitherto wholly owned. Organisations should also try to understand what they are good at and where they could benefit from external input. For example:

- Are they good at product development?
- Are they good at manufacturing?
- Are they good are distribution and selling?

2 Take account of the changing marketplace

Take a good look at your organisation in relation to its sector and market position. Gain an understanding of who is emerging as a market leader and why; which market trends are beginning to dominate; and which way things are likely to develop in the future. The organisation's stakeholders – customers, employees, shareholders and suppliers – provide an invaluable resource that can be tapped into during the data-gathering exercise.

Carry out a SWOT analysis and look at how you got where you are. Do you need to invest in your technological base, in your processing capacity, or in new markets? Does market stability – or volatility – make that investment affordable or desirable? Consider what other organisations are doing to compete on innovation, service and value for the customer. Consider verifying industry profitability by carrying out an analysis based on Porter's five forces.

3 Determine where you want to be in the future

This may well mean rethinking the business you are in or adjusting your business focus to concentrate on your core strengths. If you want to express a clear vision for the future, it is important not to be locked into the thinking of the past. The vision should be shared by everyone in the organisation as the agreed driving force that energises the business.

4 Look closely at your organisation's processes

When considering a strategic partner, you must be fully aware of what it is really like within your own organisation. Try to get a knowledgeable perspective on:

- programmes for continuing improvement and development
- policies and practices for releasing authority and encouraging initiative
- generation, analysis and use of key information
- ability to respond to changes in the marketplace.

Identify the key processes at which you are, or need to be, best. Identify the skills that you need to develop and improve. Gaining excellence in a core competence is something that requires years of consistent endeavour and application. This requires updating and renewing, but provides probably the greatest bargaining power in negotiating a strategic partnering agreement.

Action checklist: structuring the strategic partnership

1 Decide on the field of cooperation

There are three types of strategic partnership:

- **Horizontal partnerships** are usually formed with former competitors from the same industry as the partnering organisation. Collaborations in research and development usually come under this umbrella.

- **Vertical partnerships** are usually formed with organisations in the supply-delivery chain, such as suppliers, marketers or distributors.

- **Diagonal partnerships** are created with organisations from other industries. A good example would be a public/private-sector partnership to build a hospital.

In each case, complementary core competencies, strategic business fit and ability to trust the other party are the principal issues that should be considered in the decision-making process.

2 Decide on the level of cooperation

Consider:

- what time frames are optimal for getting the project operational
- the resources that can be allocated to the project
- how formal the structural arrangements between partners need to be – the legal form of organisation, process and communication procedures, control processes and organisational structure itself.

3 Decide on the level of involvement

To restrict the agreement to two partners may or may not be satisfactory. You can create a memorandum of understanding that paves the way for future opportunities for collaboration. Strategically, innovation, production or delivery may benefit from establishing relationships with more than one partner, each bringing their own expertise and expanding the richness and potential of the collaboration. In this case the partnership will evolve from a two-way partnership to a dynamic network of contributors. The addition of each new partner, however, increases the risks of something going wrong.

4 Decide on measurement and control issues

All strategic partnerships need some form of control. Make sure you have the governance structure to manage this process. You must determine:

- which activities each partner will control
- how much control each partner will exercise
- how control will be exercised.

It would be ideal for partners to have similar measurement systems, but this is unlikely to be the case. Contributions to, and outcomes from, the partnership may be difficult to apportion precisely when marketing, quality targets and learning objectives are key contributors to financial goals.

Action checklist: selecting the appropriate partner

1 Identify intra- or extra-industry players for basic fit

This is largely a question of information-gathering and analysis. Having decided on a horizontal, vertical or diagonal approach, search out the leading or emerging players that can add their strength to yours in a win-win situation. Bear in mind such questions as:

- What are the risks in such a collaboration and how are they spread between the partners?
- Does this potential partner have a hidden agenda?
- Is the potential partner able to fulfil the required role?
- How turbulent is the existing/future market?
- Are there other collaborators or associates in the game?
- In the event of problems, how quickly could we remove or replace the partner?

Public/private-sector partnerships can sometimes involve multibillion-dollar projects. The selection of partners is critical to avoid budget and time overruns and maximise success.

2 Establish a partnering champion

The partnering champion should be a senior manager who commands respect at all levels, has keen powers of analysis and gets things done. The champion will be responsible for laying the framework for the partnership agreement, spreading the 'ownership' of the partnership and making it work in the start-up phase.

3 Examine strategic fit

Broad business focus is much more important than short-term goals, so make sure that the partnership fits with overall planning and will not cause a detour or even a U-turn. A harmonious business focus will lay the foundation for common belief systems, business plans, partnership structures and time scales.

4 Beware of hidden dangers

Cultural incompatibility may lurk beneath the surface of many potentially successful partnerships. Management style, organisational 'feel' and the way things really get done in an organisation are not easy to quantify and even more difficult to assimilate. It is inadvisable and, in any case, well-nigh impossible to impose cultural norms from the outside. The potential problem analysis (PPA) method, part of Charles Kepner and Benjamin Tregoe's approach to problem solving, can be used to identify areas of risk and identify measures to mitigate them.

As a manager you should avoid:

- forgetting the importance of cultural fit
- ignoring areas of potential conflict
- underestimating the resources required (time, money and effort) for major projects.

And remember to:

- focus on business logic rather than short-term gain
- identify critical issues and potential obstacles
- build in flexible monitoring and measurement processes.

Developing new products

In business and engineering, new product development (NPD) is the term used to describe the complete process of bringing a new product or service to market. It embraces the conception, generation, analysis, development, testing, marketing and commercialisation of new products. This NPD life cycle is also known as a phased or sequential implementation model.

Alternative models of NPD fall into two broad categories:

- accelerating time to market
- integrated activities to achieve both flexibility and acceleration of development.

In the rapidly changing environments characterising most industries today, proficiency in the process of product innovation is necessary for organisational survival. Given that environmental change requires organisational adaptation, new product innovation models can be expected to appear in response to new competitive landscapes.

New products and services are the lifeblood of all businesses. Investing in their development is not an optional extra – it is crucial to business growth and profitability. However, embarking on the development process is risky. Careful planning and organisation are required.

This checklist looks at product innovation models. It sets down the phased steps of the sequential implementation model and juxtaposes this traditional cycle with accelerating time-to-market models or integrated implementation models. In practice some of these stages may overlap, but the presence of a staged process will help keep timing and costs under control.

Action checklist

1 Phased or sequential implementation models

Traditional models of NPD are classified under the heading of stage-gate models. The NPD process is divided into a number of stages, which are themselves composed of a group of predetermined, related and often parallel activities. At each stage, the details of how to perform each task as well as various best practices are specified. To pass on to the next stage, a potential new product has to pass a decision 'gate'. Each gate forms a set of criteria by which the project is judged. The stage-gates will eliminate all but those projects most likely to succeed. The gates common to phased implementation models usually follow this sequence.

2 Idea generation

Ideas can come from many sources, in many ways and involve different types of people. Sources of ideas may include:

- market research into customer 'wants'
- creativity sessions, e.g. brainstorming, lateral thinking
- research and development
- employee ideas, e.g. from the sales force or through suggestion schemes
- existing, abandoned and discontinued products
- technological developments, e.g. licensing, monitoring the technical literature
- observing and building on competitor activity.

Consider all sources to start with. Research has shown that

from a possible seven new ideas aimed at the generation of new products, six will fail during the screening, analysis, R&D and testing phases.

3 Idea screening

Screening involves pitching new ideas against organisational objectives to test whether they are compatible with, support or enhance/fit into your business's strategic plans. Ideas judged unsuitable can be eliminated at this stage. Criteria to use might include:

- technical feasibility
- potential profitability
- corporate/strategic fit
- production cost
- product life
- competitive advantage
- sustainability
- environmental/regulatory fit
- socio/political considerations.

Ideas screened out at this stage should not be discarded, however. Market or technology changes may turn them into potential successes in the future or you may be able to license the idea outside the organisation.

Ideas that are clearly innovative and could have significant market potential should be protected by filing a patent application. This may require further work, including the development of prototypes and pilot schemes, but the establishment of ownership is becoming increasingly important in a business environment where knowledge and information are key sources of competitive advantage.

4 Analyse the market

This stage turns an idea into a recognisable product concept and identifies its attributes and market position/potential. It involves testing the concept against possible target markets and customer needs to see whether the idea in development could be improved on. This analysis should indicate possible sales and production costs, thereby giving a better idea of the risks involved and the product's potential. Customers may also suggest uses for the product that had not been anticipated. It is important that results should be viewed objectively – do not ignore results that seem to contradict your original impressions.

Make sure products and services are matched to market needs. New products and services have to offer benefits that meet your customers' needs. You need to discover what these are. Market research, using techniques such as surveys and focus groups, will help you do this.

Consider consumer and market trends. For example:

- Are you entering a growing, established or declining market?
- Are population demographics significant?
- Does telecommunications technology have a key role to play?
- How is demand affected by environmental and sustainability issues?

Remember that although the end user of your product or service might be your most important customer, you may have to take the needs of other parties into account.

5 Analyse potential competitors

Once an idea has passed the initial market analysis, the next stage is to identify any potential rivals for the market niche you are targeting, so a competitor analysis will be needed. You must not only meet customer needs but also do so in a way that is better than the alternatives offered by the competition.

Your new product or service needs a unique selling proposition

– a feature or characteristic that makes it stand out in the marketplace. Before entering the market you need to determine:

- How are customer needs currently being met?
- Why would customers choose your products or services rather than those of your competitors, both now and in the future?
- What risks are you prepared to take to launch into this market?

Competitor analysis may also lead to the identification of possible collaborators who may help to accelerate product development or distribution, or improve market impact or penetration. Sources of information include:

- market research and stockbroker reports
- trade and consumer publications
- trade associations
- universities, research and professional institutions
- information available publicly on the internet.

6 Embark on the research and development phase

Once a project has cleared the first four stages, the ideas behind it need to be turned into a product that the identified market has helped to define. Design is crucial as it can make or break the product.

A first prototype, pilot service or laboratory samples may be used for testing initial customer reaction, leading to possible changes or improvements.

7 Start production

A pilot is often carried out to test the feasibility of the manufacturing process before scaling up to full production. Ensure the quality of your product. Test every feature separately and then the product as a whole to make sure it conforms to the specifications and performs as it should – for example, a machine is reliable, food products are not harmful, services are deliverable on the scale required. You may choose to use an independent facility for testing, such as a commercial laboratory or research foundation.

8 Test the market and finalise the concept

Test marketing of the product in small-scale tests with consumers can provide information about the potential success of the product and marketing programme, thereby limiting the risk involved. Agree on a marketing strategy so that all the elements in the marketing mix can be tested. This stage can identify improvements to be made in advertising, promotion, distribution and pricing, or it may result in a decision to halt the project. Test marketing can be an expensive exercise so use it wisely. Not all products are test marketed, especially where they involve little risk.

There are three basic test market strategies:

- **National replication** – the national launch plans are scaled down and tested in a few representative cities. Bear in mind, however, that this differs from a nationwide introduction.

- **Experimentation** – the product is tried out in specific retail outlets. However, this allows for few variations in marketing strategies.

- **Behavioural model-based analysis** – this approach collects the information necessary to compensate for problems in national replication and an analysis is made using a detailed model of consumer behaviour to enable forecasts of the effects of modifying marketing strategies.

There are various methods for analysis, such as panel data projection models and continuous flow models. It is important to select the most appropriate model for the specific test market analysis and budget.

9 Launch the product

The test-marketing phase will have helped refine the marketing campaign involving the 4 Ps – product and price definition, place (target market) and promotion. The marketing policy should specify the long-term objectives and provide a broad outline of how these are to be achieved. The timing of the launch must be planned carefully and the business environment monitored so that the launch plan can be revised to take account of any changes.

10 Distribute the product

The product must be available where and when customers may want it, but the extent of availability must be balanced against the cost. There are a number of approaches (channels to market) that a company can take, such as distribution direct to the customer or via intermediaries such as agents, wholesalers and retailers.

Distribution channel design will depend on:

- the product – for example, whether it is perishable, whether it is an industrial or consumer product
- the product's customers
- the geographical spread
- the cost.

Identifying the appropriate channels to market, and understanding their cost and availability and how to work them, are crucial to a successful product launch. The importance of this is often underestimated.

11 Reinvent the product

Demanding customers and increasing competition cause product obsolescence, so what was once an original premium-priced innovation can rapidly become an off-the-shelf commodity. The cycle therefore begins again with product generation.

Various models follow this phased or sequential implementation

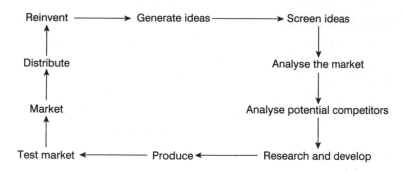

Figure 6: NPD process model

pattern, the most established of which include the Booz, Allen and Hamilton model and Kotler's model.

Whether the activities in the NPD process (see Figure 6) need to be followed in a step-by-step sequence is open to question. In the development of some high-tech products it may be beneficial to undertake the tasks in parallel – for example steps 6 and 7 – to reduce risk on the one hand and time to market on the other. The creative nature of NPD may also undermine the validity of the sequential approach.

Stages 5–8 may overlap, but critically it is these stages that may have slowed down the NPD life cycle and led to the emergence of other, faster models described below.

12 Measure and monitor the success of NPD initiatives

As with any process, it is important to continually monitor the performance of NPD procedures and systems. This provides evidence on how well the system is functioning and enables you to consider if and where improvements can be made.

Time to market is a measure that can be broken down into the various gated stages. It can also be helpful to keep track of the number of ideas entering and exiting each stage; remember, however, that not all ideas will be carried through to completion. A more strategic measure is the percentage of revenue earned from new products developed over, say, the past two years, compared with total revenue. For high-performing, innovative companies this can be as much as 100%.

It is also interesting to track expenditure on NPD compared with total expenditure. Bear in mind that costs will grow as a project progresses through the various stages and that the potential for flexibility in concept or design is highest in the early stages of the process.

Other NPD models

Accelerating time to market

In commerce, time to market (TTM) is the length of time it takes from a product being conceived to its being available for sale. TTM is important in industries where products quickly become outmoded. A common assumption is that TTM matters most for first-of-a kind products, but actually the leader often has the luxury of time, while the clock is clearly running for the followers.

TTM generation dates back to the mid-1980s; its primary focus is developing individual products faster. These models provide an overall timescale for NPD that incorporates both development time and time to launch. There are eight 'time' elements so that opportunities for maximum efficiency and improvement can be identified. These comprise the time needed to:

- understand the market needs
- harness appropriate technologies
- understand a concept that is technically and commercially sound
- develop concepts to a functioning and producible design
- mobilise the manufacturing facilities and processes
- ramp up production volumes
- deliver and fulfil orders
- maintain or service a product.

Many people assume that TTM is improved (shortened) by skipping steps of the development process, thus compromising quality. Those who use highly structured development processes, such as stage-gate or Six Sigma, view NPD as a sequence of steps to be followed. Skipping a step, because of time pressure, for example, not only undercuts quality but also can lengthen development time if steps need to be completed or repeated later. According to this view, TTM is improved by following all the prescribed steps.

Product and cycle-time excellence

The product and cycle-time excellence model (PACE) incorporates elements of all three categories: sequential, time to market and integration.

This version of a stage-gate model was developed by Theodore Pittiglio, Robert Rabin, Robert Todd and Michael McGrath in 1992. Elements include the phase review process; core teams; structured development; process, product strategy; technology management; design techniques and development tools; cross-project management. The first three elements represent the tools that are required for each product development project; the last four are process support elements. The advantages of PACE include:

- the use of a structured new product methodology, allowing review points to be inserted between the various phases in the process
- blurred divisions between the phases and review points, so that phases can overlap
- the strategic direction of the company being taken into account at each stage of the process
- the use of cross-functional teams to increase flexibility and save time
- the opportunity for senior management to balance the risk to the company resulting from breakthrough projects, against the lesser risk of derivative projects.

Integrated implementation

Integrated models are often based on traditional phased development models but have been modified to suit individual organisations and to speed up the development process. Practices that slow down product development, such as mandatory phase reviews, are often abandoned.

Integrative models reinforce the shift from structure to processes. Many modern organisations do not operate on a process basis; rather, they are functional and hierarchical and suffer from isolated departments, poor coordination and limited lateral communication. The shift is also from functions to knowledge. Instead of thinking in terms of distinct departments that come together to take an idea from inception to launch, the rationale of integrative models is to think in terms of the pool of knowledge required to deliver a product.

Design for manufacturability and assembly

Design for manufacturability and assembly (DFMA) is a cross-functional team approach to NPD. Representatives from each function involved in the product development and launch process are included in a development team from the product's inception.

The product development process is divided into six stages with overlap and parallel processing built into the model:

- product design
- process design/engineering
- manufacturing
- marketing
- sales and distribution
- related functions, such as customer care.

The contribution of manufacturing and assembly personnel from the beginning of the project allows the early identification of time, labour and materials saving measures and avoids delays caused by inadequate process design. DFMA also provides a number of design guidelines that can simplify product manufacture and decrease the time and costs involved.

Multi-function project management

The multi-function project management model was developed to enable shorter time-to-market and market-driven research and development. It identifies four project phases to be conducted in parallel, with considerable overlap between phases three and four:

● market requirement specification

● feasibility study and project preparation

● development and test

● market introduction.

Five competence areas required in the development of new products are also identified:

● service (e.g. help desks and warranty provision)

● sourcing (e.g. materials and purchasing)

● engineering (e.g. design and testing)

● marketing (e.g. pre-sales support, market introduction)

● logistics (e.g. forecasting and inventory management).

The five competence areas are represented in a multifunctional team from the beginning of the project and work is undertaken in each competence area simultaneously. Decision points are inserted at certain phases in the development process to check whether the project should be continued and whether it should progress to the next step.

Framework for innovation and flexibility in high-technology firms

Five basic tier groups are involved in this model:

● target customers

- product design
- product marketing
- product manufacturing
- product management.

These five tiers are involved in four cooperative triads, each of which represents a different phase in the evolution of the product, and during which three of the five are directly involved with each other:

- The inception triad (product management, target customer and product marketing groups) gains a perception of market acceptance, pricing, volume and packaging.

- The feasibility triad (product management, target customer and product design groups) involves design flexibility and the fulfilment of the new product's feature list with focus on applicable technologies.

- The realisability triad (product management, product design and product manufacturing groups) centres on aspects of plant capacity, flexibility and technical expertise, and asks if the product can actually be made.

- The distributing triad (product management, product manufacturing and product marketing groups) addresses questions of packaging, transport and distribution, and sales.

As a manager you should avoid:

- leaving market research too late
- moving on to the development stage before agreeing the product definition
- underestimating the strengths and weaknesses of the competition.

Deciding whether to outsource

Outsourcing is generally understood to mean the retention of responsibility for services by an organisation that has devolved the day-to-day delivery of those services to an external organisation, usually under a contract with agreed performance standards, costs and conditions.

In this checklist the organisation considering outsourcing some or part of its functions will be called the organisation, and the external organisation that is taking them on will be called the agency.

Outsourcing has evolved into a strategic option for businesses of all sizes. Often seen as a threat by employees and an opportunity by organisations, outsourcing has become standard practice in many businesses. Its focus has moved from the shifting of processes to locally based third-party agencies towards more global offshoring and outsourcing of entire functional areas, such as human resources.

On the surface, the benefits of outsourcing seem both straightforward and considerable. As well as cost savings, there are many other elements that lead managers to consider outsourcing, such as the need for flexibility both to deal with rises and falls in product demand and to improve ways of delivering products or services. Experience shows, however, that outsourcing has pitfalls, dangers and costs, and needs to be carefully managed to retain a strong degree of control over outsourced services.

This checklist is intended to assist those making decisions on whether, what and how to outsource. It encompasses stages in the outsourcing process leading up to drawing up and testing a contract. The key areas to address are highlighted, but further legal advice should be sought for all contractual and employment law issues.

Action checklist

1 Establish the outsourcing project team

Treat the outsourcing proposal as a project. Apply the principles of project management, especially in selecting a project leader and team and setting up terms of reference, method of working and an action plan.

2 Analyse your current position

Ideally, you should have carried out a radical review of your organisation's processes. You do not want to outsource an activity that might be better integrated with another you regard as 'core'. You must have a clear vision of where the business is heading and have assessed:

- the advantage to be achieved by concentrating on core services
- the minimum involvement required in things that do not affect the customer
- the control required of non-diminishing, non-productive overheads
- functions that are more viable through an external agency.

3 Pay attention to people

As soon as it becomes known that outsourcing is under consideration, people will suffer from anxiety and uncertainty. At best their working life will transfer from one employer to another; at worst their job could be lost. Keep people at the forefront of your thinking.

4 Benchmark

Someone, somewhere is probably doing the same thing in a better way, or in the same way at lower cost. Identify appropriate organisations to benchmark against and establish which activities they are outsourcing.

5 Come to a decision

Decide which are your core areas. The principal questions are:

● What is core to the business and to the future of the business?

● What can bring competitive advantage?

Then decide whether outsourcing should become a policy for organisation-wide application to non-core areas, should be used as the need arises, or should not be used at all.

6 Decide what to outsource

Logically, what you could outsource follows on from the decision process. If you focus on the core competencies of your organisation and on your uniqueness, targets for outsourcing become those areas that make up the support, administration, routine and internal servicing of the organisation.

Areas that have traditionally been candidates for outsourcing include legal services, transport, catering, printing, advertising, accounting and, especially, internal auditing and security. More recently these have been joined by data processing, IT, information processing, public relations, buildings management and training.

Staff are often transferred along with their function to the agency providing the outsourcing services. Obviously, this is an area that requires great consideration and sensitivity. It may also involve legal considerations. For example, in the UK, the Transfer of Undertaking (Protection of Employment) Regulations (TUPE) protect the terms and conditions of employees when business is transferred from one organisation to another.

7 Tender the package

The tender is both an objective document detailing the services, activities and targets required and a selling document that serves to attract potential suppliers. Outsourcing should not be seen as just a matter of getting rid of problem areas, as outsourcing these is unlikely to resolve them.

Once an attractive package has been defined, send an outline specification and request for information to those agencies likely to be interested. The outline specification should contain the broad intention of the outsourcing proposal and timescales the organisation has in mind. The request for information is a questionnaire-type eligibility test to establish the level of an agency's competence and interest. The next stage is sending an invitation to tender – a precise document spelling out what agencies should bid for.

8 Choose a partner

The tender process should be used for the evaluation of facts, but choosing an outsourcing partner is much more than choosing a new supplier, because the process involves a customised service, agreement on service levels and a contract. At this stage an organisation will be looking for an agency with which it can share objectives and values, have regular senior management meetings and disclose otherwise confidential information. Harmony of management styles is central to success. The organisation will also look for:

- a proven track record, a flexible approach and financial viability
- experience in handling the sensitive issue of staff absorption
- evidence of quality management
- how important the contract is for the agency in terms of turnover.

9 Meet the staff

If staff are to be transferred to the agency, it is essential that they are given the opportunity to meet their prospective new employer before any contracts are signed. Allowing concerns to be aired and questions to be asked may help to reduce feelings of being dumped or cast aside. However, glaring conflicts in style and personality may emerge which can have an important impact at the contractual stage. Many other issues involving terms and conditions of employment will need addressing, including those of appropriate compensation if agency employment is not available or required.

10 Draw up the contract

If the project team is to draw up the contract, it will need to have a strong legal input, relating to any legislation such as the UK TUPE Regulations 1981 as amended in 2006. As a guide, the contract should cover:

- measurable service levels the agency should provide, with checks and controls to ensure that these are met – perhaps via a liaison manager – and clauses including remedies or financial compensation required if they are not

- demarcation of service responsibilities and boundaries so that both organisation and agency are clear about who is doing what

- who owns what in terms of equipment and hardware

- the fate of the staff to be transferred and details of their terms and conditions of employment – in the short, medium and long term, including pensions provisions

- flexibility and allowance for change – for example, if business volumes double or halve

- a contract term, with a review date and provision for the function to revert to the organisation

- a pilot period before the contract becomes fully operational.

Legal advice should be sought for all contractual and employment law issues.

11 Test the contract

Make sure that the contract will stand up to the rigours and complexities of the operation in action. A period of testing and trial is ideal for making adjustments before the contract becomes final and to examine the possibility and consequences of the partnership breaking down.

As a manager you should avoid:

- losing organisational control of services that are outsourced
- letting the goal of cost savings dominate everything else
- thinking that outsourcing is the answer to all problems
- outsourcing core strategic, customer or financial management functions or operations.

And remember:

- to understand the scope of the services to be outsourced
- to have a clear vision of what outsourcing is to achieve
- that you are outsourcing an activity, but not responsibility for it.

Using consultants

The following definition is taken from the management consultancy competence framework developed by the Institute of Business Consulting, now the Institute of Consulting:

Management consulting involves individuals, whether self-employed or employed, using their knowledge and experience, and their analytical and problem-solving skills, to add value into a wide variety of organisations within a framework of appropriate and relevant professional standards, disciplines and ethics.

This checklist is intended for prospective users of consultants and suggests some of the questions they should ask themselves before commissioning an assignment, as well as advice on getting the most from a consultancy relationship. Buying in and using management consultancy can be a valuable investment providing you:

- allow enough time for the assignment
- carefully define the area of need
- know what you want the consultant to do
- take care in selecting the right consultant
- manage the relationship effectively
- monitor progress towards desired outcomes
- do not become overdependent on the consultant
- try to achieve knowledge transfer as part of the process.

There are many advantages in using consultants, including their expertise. As they are immersed in their specialism, they are well-placed to advise on the state of the art in your industry. It may be impractical for an organisation to tap such expertise in any other way. Other advantages are:

● it may be more cost-effective to buy in expertise for short-term projects as and when it is needed

● help may be required for an overstretched management team or to pursue a project that would otherwise not be completed

● outsiders can see things that are unclear to those on the inside and say things that staff members may fear to articulate. Equally, employees may be more willing to agree to a course of action if they know that impartial advice has been taken.

Action checklist

1 Clarify the need to buy in external expertise

Do you really need a management consultant? Check that the knowledge and expertise required is not already available within the organisation. Consider also that if ongoing expertise is needed, it may be more cost-effective to employ someone with the necessary experience. If you are looking at a short-term project or you need the objective perspective of an outsider, a consultancy assignment may offer the best way forward.

2 Involve the senior management from the beginning

Gain the approval of senior managers for the decision to use consultants and keep them informed during the selection process. This will help ensure that your choice of consultant will be accepted at the top level.

3 Understand organisational procurement policy and practice in respect of hiring consultants

Large organisations often require procurement departments to manage the hiring process. In the UK, public-sector organisations may have rigorous controls in place, require contracts to be put out to tender, or need to follow the guidance of the Office of Government Commerce. Bear in mind, however, that buying commodities (such as stationery and computers) is very different from buying services and intellectual property. Be aware of the risks of bureaucratising and depersonalising the selection process. Question assumptions made by procurers and procedures that concentrate on lowest price and that automatically employ formal invitations to tender, even when the value of the contract is small.

4 Ensure impartiality

Make sure that that any person with an interest declares this and is not part of the appointing committee or group.

5 Prepare a shortlist of possible consultants

There are various directories and registers available for identifying consultants. Some consultancies offer a wide range of services; others specialise in particular industries, in certain areas of business activity or in organisations. Recommendation is also commonly used. Ask those you work with to suggest people they trust. Make sure you request references from previous clients to establish a consultant's track record and follow them up.

6 Ask for written proposals from consultants on your shortlist

This will enable you to establish the extent to which the consultant can help you, the likely benefits and the duration of the assignment. It should also give you an insight into the consultant's approach to the problem.

7 Generate a genuine dialogue

Aim for a dialogue in a partnership sense rather than having a sharp division of labour. Rather than present consultants with a tightly defined problem, it may be helpful to engage them at the problem definition stage. They may have useful insights and strategic abilities to offer.

8 Understand the commercial imperative in consultants' minds

To win a contract, a consultant may appear to agree with your diagnosis, but may not actually do so. Once engaged, a consultant may hope to redefine the assignment – either to fit their analysis of the issue or to enable them to do what they are best at doing. Be aware, too, that once the assignment starts the work may be left to junior consultancy staff or personnel may change during the project. You may wish to stipulate that you should approve any changes of personnel. Most consultants have a follow-on contract in mind and this can colour their advice – they may tell you what you want to hear and not what you need to hear.

9 Study the consultancy proposals submitted

These should include:

- an understanding of the situation or need
- a programme of work
- a timetable for completing the work
- a statement of benefits
- an indication of the consultant's style and approach
- details of staff, including relevant qualifications and experience
- the resources required, time, information, equipment – and the time of your own staff, for meetings, interviews and work in joint teams, for example
- references to previous work of a similar nature undertaken elsewhere
- estimates of fees and costs.

10 Finalise the agreement

Check the terms and conditions of the agreement carefully to make sure that they are clear and unambiguous and that you are happy with the provisions, especially if you do not have a standard contract for consultancy assignments. You may wish to refer to the standard terms and conditions for consultancy contracts available from the Institute of Consulting.

11 Take care if you need to employ more than one consultant

Sometimes a job will require more than one consultant, for example if specialist knowledge that the main (or 'lead') consultant cannot supply is needed. Make sure that any such relationship is clearly defined, and in particular that it is clear who is employing, managing, instructing and evaluating the secondary consultant. The lead consultancy may not have the skills to evaluate or monitor the specialist, in which case it may fall to you as the client, but this does not mean that you must assume all responsibility for the subcontractor. You may need to accept an additional overhead to make sure that specialist elements of the project are properly completed; build this into your evaluation system for the overall project. Make sure that the contract sets out clearly where these responsibilities lie. This will probably be a statement that the lead contractor is liable for any problems with subcontractors and their work.

12 Explain to all concerned why a consultant is being employed

Brief staff on why a consultant has been appointed; when the consultant will arrive; and the cooperation that is expected. Consider appointing someone as the main contact with the consultant, for example to help them with unfamiliar routines, geography and so on.

13 Ask for regular reports and meetings on the progress of the assignment

It is important to monitor progress and measure it against agreed objectives and programmes of work. You may wish to ask for regular reports or exception reports, and to schedule meetings regularly at key points during the consultation period: start-up, midway and project end, for example. If any problems arise, a face-to-face meeting can help to resolve them quickly and amicably.

14 Have a debriefing session before the end of the assignment

Make sure that the consultant summarises the findings and conclusions of the project either in a report or in a presentation. Make sure that there are no misunderstandings or errors and that you have received what you asked for.

15 Assess the consultant's effectiveness

When implementing change, either during or after consultancy, check that recommendations and outcomes are properly applied and that they are not being undermined by a return to 'business as usual'. Discuss any particular difficulties that arise during implementation with those concerned. Regularly examine the results being achieved and consider follow-up visits from the consultant at appropriate intervals after completion of the project.

As a manager you should avoid:

- assuming that staff will readily accept an outside expert – be prepared to manage any staff resentment that may arise when employing a consultant
- being unprepared to manage any adverse reactions
- losing sight of objectives
- becoming overly reliant on a consultant

- becoming embroiled in the consultant's internal management issues, such as managing subcontractors – unless this has been agreed with the lead supplier

- being led by consultants to extend the consulting assignment beyond its original scope – unless this has been agreed as valuable and approved by the senior management team.

Acknowledgements

The Chartered Management Institute (CMI) would like to thank the members of our Subject Matter Experts group for their generous contribution to the development of the management checklists. This panel of over 60 members and fellows of CMI and its sister institute, the Institute of Consulting, draw on their knowledge and expertise to provide feedback on the currency, relevance and practicality of the advice given in the checklists. A full listing of the subject matter experts is available at www.managers.org.uk/subject-matter-experts.

This book has been made possible by the work of CMI's staff, in particular Catherine Baker, Piers Cain, Sarah Childs, Michelle Jenkins, Linda Lashbrooke, Robert Orton, Nick Parker, Karen Walsh and not least Mary Wood, the Series Editor. We would also like to thank Stephen Brough, Paul Forty and Clare Grist Taylor of Profile Books for their support.

The management checklists are based on resources available online at www.managers.org.uk to CMI members to assist them in their work and career development, and to subscribers to the online resource portal ManagementDirect.

Index